Chapman 104

Centenary Issue Part 3 (of 3)

Editorial 2

Three Prose Pieces
Hugh MacDiarmid 4

Poems: Raymond Vettese 11

Meg Bateman 15

Jamie Reid Baxter 17

With Tormad
Ian Stephen 18

Rediscovered Poems and Prose
Hugh MacDiarmid 21

Disney Exist
Alastair Sim 35

Poems: Rob MacKenzie 38

Leaving
Jenni Daiches 43

Poems: David Kinloch 50

Unpublished in *Lucky Poet*
Hugh MacDiarmid 55

Poems: Diana Hendry 60

Andrew Philip 63

Roddy Lumsden 66

Winston Churchill
Mark Barbieri 68

Poems: Lydia Robb 72

Poems etc: Iain Galbraith 76

Stardust Disco
Gavin Bowd 80

Poems: aonghas macneacail .. 82

The Language of Poetry
Franco Loi 89

Poem: Thorbjørn Campbell ... 98

Proverbs!: Brent Hodgson 99

Poems: Donald Smith 102

Last Tango in Glasgow
Jack Withers 108

Poems: David C Purdie 113

Dauvit Horsbroch 115

Two Short Stories
Iain Crichton Smith 118

Poems: Martin Bates 122

C L Vinson 125

Reviews 129

Cover: William Johnstone, A Point in Time *(1929), Scottish Gallery of Modern Art. All paintings by William Johnstone in this issue are with the kind permission of the artist's estate.*

Editorial

This issue marks the end of the *Chapman* centenary celebrations and the beginning of a new phase in the magazine's development. Issues 100-104 taken together amount to a showcase of Scottish writing over the last 30 or more years. They make a graphic representation in poetry and narrative of a spectacular evolutionary process in Scottish culture, reflected in, and to some extent, nudged along by the magazine. It's been truly exciting to observe, and be a part of, that evolution. Scottish literature, and Scottish culture generally, has changed from a neglected backwater, to being seen the world over as something unique and intensely valuable, not just the work of the last 30 years, but an accomplishment building over centuries.

It seems fitting in this final Centenary issue to remember the still-controversial figure of Hugh MacDiarmid. Thanks to the Herculean labours of John Manson, a large body of unpublished work has come to light – poems, prose pieces, letters ... Some of this is already published in Carcanet's volume, *The Revolutionary Art of the Future*. In *Chapman* 104, we reveal yet more poems, and prose items, all providing potent insights into the genius of MacDiarmid and testaments to his astonishing energies. Working on these 'new' poems, I have been deeply struck by just how far-seeing and revolutionary MacDiarmid was. So much in his work resonates powerfully today with indicators of battles still being fought. Like him or loathe him, no-one can deny his role in getting us where we are today, nor his inspiration, as a fiery catalyst, a galvanising fuse. The MacDiarmid feature is our tribute to his labours and achievement.

Who better also to celebrate here than William Johnstone, an artist with whom MacDiarmid collaborated closely over many years. Despite exhibitions in the Hayward Gallery (1981) and elsewhere, he is not nearly as recognised in the art world as MacDiarmid is in the literary sphere. I hope this small showing of his work will stimulate new interest in Johnstone, who in his own way was as remarkable and individual as MacDiarmid. Their work shares the capacity to be at once utterly rooted in the local, yet spectacularly universal in reach, moving in mood from the tender and gentle, to making the hardest hitting of political/aesthetic statements.

Heather Scott's translation of Franco Loi's thesis, 'The Language of Poetry', similarly reminds us of something which, in terms of current deconstructionist theory, might seem old fashioned. He resumes that crucial debate about the ultimate springs of poetry, exploring and contrasting the nature of the aesthetic with the mystical impulse which provides all art with its drive and focus. Critical discussion has become too confined to the academic sphere and hedged around by critical conventions. Loi's article is a breath of fresh air, and I hope this debate will continue.

Sadly, during last year, we have prematurely lost several important literary figures. Neil MacCallum, poet and ex-editor of *Lallans*, laboured tirelessly to advance many aspects of literature and language, and to develop Scotland as a nation. William Cookson was the indefatigable editor of *Agenda* – a magazine which brought the work of certain Scottish poets to the fore at a time when they were largely ignored, even in Scotland. Novelist and poet Colin Mackay is well known to *Chapman* readers, especially his poetry collection *Cold Night Lullaby* about his tragic experiences in Bosnia. A hugely talented writer, he committed suicide last summer, putting an end to a great deal of promise. Giles Gordon, novelist and literary agent, was a veritable powerhouse whose energies, enthusiasm and imagination knew no bounds – many writers owe to him success of their careers. And even Kathleen Raine's death, aged 97, was untimely. She was still highly active, full of new plans, but was ploughed down by a silly motoring accident. These deaths, and the difficult careers of such figures as MacDiarmid and Johnstone, bring home the unseen and unrecognised dangers in devoting oneself to labouring in the cultural field. It is a fraught business, involving personal sacrifice and pain, bringing stress and difficulty into areas of life which most can take for granted. One of my aims with *Chapman* has always been to work, directly and indirectly, to make it easier for writers and artists to exist in our community.

There is an enormous range of styles of writing here, literally from the sublime to the ridiculous. We publish again writers like Raymond Vettese and Lydia Robb, both regular contributors, writing eloquently in a genuine, vibrant Angus Scots. Gaelic poet and scholar Meg Bateman has appeared regularly in *Chapman* since early in her career, as has Ian Stephen who has abandoned his lighthouse-keeper job to become a full time writer. Jenni Calder, another regular, appears here with both poetry and fiction. Best known for work in the Museum of Scotland, Jenni's own writing is not sufficiently recognised. From Jack Withers we get strong political statement, Iain Galbraith, a thoughtful lyricism and from David Kinloch a poetry which is tough and challenging. Donald Smith's poem-sequence draws powerful legendary and historical roots, and from Brent Hodgson, as we now expect, comes Something Completely Different! Aonghas Macneacail, foremost Gaelic poet, is represented here by a body of poetry in English, but his critical polemic, the cut and thrust of his cultural arguments, has often provided the central plank of many a *Chapman* issue.

New voices to *Chapman* include Alastair Sim, whose short story will please neither VisitScotland nor Walt Disney, Andrew Philip with strong, provocative poetry and C L Vinson, whose poetry combines gritty urban realism with a profound idealism and sensitivity to the natural world.

Edwin Morgan has just been made Scotland's National Makar by our New Parliament. Congratulations to him. It is only a small tribute compared to the hugeness of his lifetime's contribution to our lives. For this we might even be able to forgive Follyrood and other disappointments!

I'm looking forward immensely now to the future. The Centenary has been largely a consolidation of past and present, but I hope too it shoots out arrows into the future. Organising and publishing it has been an gargantuan amount of work at a time of great personal difficulty, and I am immensely grateful to all the writers and artists who have contributed to it.

The Joys of Guddling

Hugh MacDiarmid

When I was a boy guddling was one of my principal delights and in ret-rospect it remains so. I do not know that I have done anything since that I enjoyed half so much. I am afraid it is not for a man of forty to attempt to savour it again, though I often wonder – without being able to come to any satisfactory finding – what my sensations would be were I to yield some fine afternoon to this recurrent temptation. Certainly, to elicit the material for a fair comparison, I would have to do it in the very waters I frequented as a boy – the Esk, the Ewes, the Wauchope, the Kirtle, and the Water of Milk. None of the other streams I have got to know since, in one way or another, seem to me anything like so 'guddleable'. Nor have my experiences of the seven seas ever engendered the same quality of excitement as these little rivers never failed to give.

I think this is due to the fact that with the latter danger was only turn of the wrist or of an ankle from safety. One could drown within an arm's length from land on each side. The menace was ubiquitous but well nigh indetectible; that had to be accepted if these waters were to be frequented at all. There was no question of sudden abnormal dangers – of tidal waves, waterspouts, undertows, and what not. They presented their perils without changing one iota out of their normal candid aspect; without – so to say – 'batting an eyelid'. The risk of shipwreck is a very different matter from the risk of drowning in a pool clear to the bottom and no bigger than an ordinary bath. This subtle concentration of danger in the very presence of the familiar gave a peculiar zest to these boyish outings among the riv-ers of my native environment, running (at least in the most interesting parts – they had their level stretches too) between well-wooded rocky banks, now a shining channel, now a gushing range of small waterfalls, now an alternation of shallows and whirlpools on the various time-sculp-tured levels of a succession of 'linns', a kind of geological staircase.

I have no idea whether guddling is still practised in these ancient haunts, or whether it has, in fact, ever been practised anywhere else. There seems to be no literature on the subject. And yet this is one of the most wonderful thrills in the whole range of country life. The feel of a pig's back or a dog's nose or the first time you kiss a girl is really nothing to it. Shooting, trapping, catching on hooks, and all the other devices for capturing fish, flesh, or fowl seem very minor excitements indeed to capturing a live creature with your actual hand – and when the live creature is a wily fish, endowed by nature with a superlative slipperiness, and powers of wriggling and leaping which make the effort seem like you are trying to handle lightning, and when in order to do it you have to stand knee-deep in whirling water and fumble gently under an intricately carved rock [where] it takes the whole length of your arm to reach your quarry, and then, the trout touched, contrive to get a good grip of it and suddenly throw it high and dry on the adjoining bank, it seems to me that here is the very prince of sports. It calls for a cool head, infinite resource, and a superb combination of patience and dispatch.

In a word, you must be a match for the fish themselves. They are quick-eyed creatures; they are alert to an unusual sound or movement of any sort in their watery medium; they have exceptional powers of lying low; they make a valiant fight for it when your fingers close on them, and are capable of either sliding out of the ring made by your thumb and fore-finger (tight enough it seems round their gills but impossibly narrow for their maximum girths) or feinting to do so and as you tighten this digital noose suddenly glissading away by a retrogressive movement down the palm of your hand, like lumps of ice. For they know very well that as you try to tighten the thumb-and-forefinger encirclement you are likely to relax automatically the 'purchase' you have been having between your lit-tle finger and the heel of your hand. Oh, they are cunning beggars.

It is no easy matter tickling them in the first instance. You must have just the right touch – a 'lucky hand' – and that can only be acquired by expe-rience, plus a good deal of natural aptitude in the first place. That is hered-itary, too; it is in the blood. It simplifies matters, of course, if at the psychological moment you can jam the trout, bottom, top, or off side, against a portion of its sheltering rock but you have to know all these fan-tastically-scooped rocks well for that or you may find that something in their shape when you attempt the 'jam' throws your hand into a less effec-tive position for maintaining its hold, or that you push too far under and instead of reaching a little back-wall of rock against which you can press your captive and consolidate your grip, there isn't any such little back-wall – in which case you probably over-balance and in trying to 'catch yourself' release the fish. Your balance is often very precarious in any case; and you have to be wary for more reasons than one of thus over-reaching yourself. And then, if you do succeed in seizing your fish and 'yanking' it out, have you made the necessary instantaneous calculation, or got some instinct operating even more subtly than that, to ensure that you made a good toss? A wild blind throw is no use. You will probably land your trout into the overhanging branches of a tree whence a moment's flapping will relieve it and let it come twirling down through the air again and into the water and off before you can attempt a catch. They are lively beasts. Apart from trees, if the river is running between rocky walls it is often no easy matter to throw a fish into such a position that it cannot wriggle back into water – even if it has to do a considerable amount of slithering over the rocks – before you can scramble up and secure it and give its head the necessary tap to put an end to its activities.

That, then, is guddling. We used to practise an inferior method called 'girning' too, which consisted in the use of a lithe rod with a running noose of rabbit-snare wire at its tip. The idea was to slip the noose over the fish's body and then jerk it out. But that was only possible when the fish was lying in open water – 'wholly surrounded by water', like an island: you couldn't 'girn' a wily creature only showing its ivory beak and having the rest of its body 'doggo' in a three-sided slot of rock. I always preferred guddling.

I suppose, if boys do it today, they do it in bathing pants, or naked per-haps. We used to roll our 'breeks' up to our thighs and our shirt-sleeves to our armpits. I still fancy I would prefer that. One or the other came down at the most awkward moments, which added to the fun. Or you went a trifle out of your depth and your breek-bottom got soaked; that heavy cold sensation actually added to the pleasure of the occasion. And to slip and go over the head in a pool is a very tame affair if you are naked or have only a pair of bathing pants on, compared with getting a pair of tweed-trousers, and a shirt, thoroughly water-logged, and having to trudge two or three miles home like a water-rat on land leave. We boys of the Scottish Borders in these old days were all perfectly amphibian in the summer months at least – amphibian so far as fresh water is concerned which is an entirely different matter from the salty buoyancy of the sea. Sea-water always seems to me so insipid in comparison.

NLS MS27061 ff. 1-10

John James Milroy

Verhaeran, the Belgian poet, has written a great deal about the insatiable animality of his country-folk but we Scots, especially those of us who are Borderers, can give the Belgians plenty of points in regard to that. We are a leaner, harder, wilder, more restless and reckless race; but the quality of our animality, though fierier than theirs, differs from it as one strong drink differs from another – as brandy from whisky, or rum from gin. Spirits today cost a great deal more and are a great deal poorer than they were in the heyday of my youth; and, though there is no less lust among us than ever, it is not the same thing at all – it lacks life. The reason for this, of course, is the decline of religion; the fleshpots of Egypt need to be well seasoned with the fear of God. That's where our folk had the great advan-tage in the old days. They were great religionists – and great sinners. The two things kept a perpetual edge on each other.

It is difficult to give you the precise flavour of our Border temper in this connection; but I can tell you a story or two that have a certain smack of it. Very typical, for instance, was the remark of a local farmer who, going out into his stackyard, found his young son – a lad in his early teens – busy in illicit intercourse behind a hayrick with a servant lassie. He surveyed the scene for a moment or two; and then, shaking his head, said: "Ye're an awfu' lad, Jock. You'll be smokin' next."

Equally true to life was the advice bawled to me one night when I was staying at a farm-house out the Wauchope Road. A young farmer from Ewes was there too, who knew I was sweet on the daughter of the house. Towards midnight he made a move to go and thinking I'd be going too, for I lived in the little town half-way between that farm and the one he was going to, he said: "Come on, then. Let's off". But I told him I was staying

7

there overnight. He laughed, and we went to the door to see him off. "Good night to ye a'", he cried, and then, turning to me, let fly with this Parthian shot, "and as for you, see that you dinna blaw on your nose in the blankets!"

We began early in that little town and though we were very, very carefully brought up indeed – and had to go to Church twice every Sunday as well as to Sunday School and Bible Class – there was little or nothing we didn't know – boys and girls alike – by the time we [were] nine or ten. I remember a lad in my own class, a farmer's son, having intercourse with big Jess Watt, the daughter of the 'Red Lion' hotelkeeper, on a desk-top one day in school, in front of us all when the teacher had gone out for a few minutes. So you see. That was the sort of children we were.

The Provost of the burgh at that time was an elderly grocer; one of the daintiest looking, indeed dandiest looking, old men you ever saw. Spick and span wasn't the word for it. He had an ethereally white face – white as his trim little silver moustache and the little silver rim of hair at the base of his skull, all the rest of which was perfectly bald and shone with a wonderful radiance. Great was the sensation when he had to retire into private life. I knew some of the boys concerned myself. After that he went up and down the street like a ghost – speaking to nobody – but as spry and finical as ever. I never see a ball of lard but I think of that old Provost: for when he used to stand in his shopdoor on a sunny day and there was a ball of lard in his window, it needed very sharp eyes to tell which was it and which was his head, of which, indeed, the ball of lard might well have been just the reflection.

I mention the old Provost and these other things about our early sexual knowledge and propensities for two reasons; the latter to show you that if something unspeakably evil seemed to me as a lad of about fourteen to be associated with a stranger, it was not because I was unaware of more ordinary vices and apt to find something peculiarly vicious in what actually arose from a common enough cause – and the former because when I did experience this sensation of something unthinkably terrible, I at once thought I saw a fleeting resemblance between the man who inspired me with it and the old Provost. And yet the old Provost himself had never given me that feeling of horrible depravity.

This stranger was called John James Milroy. His old father and mother lived in a solitary house at the end of a long lane leading down by the side of the railway line to one of the local tweed-mills. Their house was a sort of lodge to that isolated factory and old Milroy, a big-bodied, broad-faced old man with a square white beard, was an overseer in the mill and also acted as a sort of night watchman. He and his wife, and their elderly spinster daughter Jane, were members of our Church; and though it was too far for the old folk to come to it often, Jane was a particularly active member and so was a great deal in contact with my father and mother. But I had never seen – or, indeed, heard of – her brother before, and I gathered from the whisperings and significant looks my father and mother exchanged about him that there was something very mysterious about him – that he was, at least, the black sheep of the family. But I could not glean anything about the precise nature of his wickedness.

I did not see him for about a fortnight after he came to the town, for he did not attend Church on the intervening Sunday – or, indeed, on any subsequent Sunday. But I was sent to give a message to his sister and was invited in – and there he was and I was introduced to him. The very sight of him gave me the shivers – but there was nothing in his appearance to inspire a feeling of revulsion, and I thought that it was probably only my anticipations that caused it. He was a tallish man of about forty, a trifle too stout, and too puffy about the face, but dressed extremely well, in a quiet gentlemanly way and yet with a touch of nattiness for which my eyes failed to account. But, though it was summer-time and he was indoors anyway, he wore gloves on both his hands – and, for some reason or other, shaking hands with him gave me a horrible feeling. His gloved hand seemed as light as cork. It gave no grip. The only other thing I noticed – and I noticed it more and more every time I saw him after that – was the way he moved; every movement he made seemed made with infinite care, an extraordinary slow motion effect. If he turned his head it seemed to take ages and one felt that if anything made him jerk suddenly it would fly right off the neck. I saw him again and again in the streets after that and it was always just as if a slow motion shot had got mixed up with a lively reel.

Literary Impersonations

Sherwood Anderson's 'No Swank' gives his impressions of well-known people. I may be expected to give here my impressions of some of the better-known figures in the Scottish literary movement. I shall do so with becoming brevity. As it happens I have a ready way of doing this since I have at intervals in recent years amused myself playing 'Britton', a popular parlour game of New York and Hollywood for some time after Kenneth Britton began displaying his novel 'psychological portraiture' of film stars – Mae West, a radiator twined with red roses resting on two white kid curlers, all enclosed in a beer 'schooner'; Myrna Loy's portrait in matches, wheat, four insects, and a doll whose skirt is a deflated balloon; Jean Harlow composed of a handful of cotton emerging from a cup, a silver spoon filled with pins, and some green poker chips. Mr Britton spends at least a week (I only spend a weak moment now and again) on each of his 'portraits' in objects. First he analyses the person and visualises the display. Then he chases all over town, searching jewellers' shops, department stores, and ten-cent stores for the necessary articles. With painstaking care he cements the objects onto a base, covering the exhibit with glass. Some are set in round domes, others in square cases, while a few are small plaques of flat or small things.

In my little show, Eric Linklater is in a big round dome, of course, and Edwin Muir is on an extremely small plaque of very flat and exceedingly small things. That will be understood. But it is difficult to 'suggest' one's subject in this way to people not already familiar with the appearance of the writer in question. Linklater, for example, is represented by an egg and a pair of spectacle lenses so arranged as to suggest the wheels of a bicycle. The egg should be in the saddle, of course, but there is no saddle, so instead of an egg scorching on a bicycle like a pair of spectacles gone mad, the effect is of an incomplete bicycle nonchalantly going nowhere with the rider the egg – unconsciously fallen through and mixed up with the works.

George Blake is represented by a black sugar pig stood in a Napoleon-on-the-HMS Bellerophon attitude before a miniature microphone.

Most of the plaques are blank but with different names underneath – Ian MacPherson, Edward Albert, James Barke, and so on.

Neil Gunn is represented by a stuffed canary with a miniature whisky-bottle joyously uplifted in one foot. A little distance away is a small aloof crystalline egg.

Compton MacKenzie is a paper of pins, and several safety pins, on a gramophone record balanced on the claws of a stuffed kitten.

A G MacDonnell is the same as Eric Linklater without the egg.

One plaque with a stave of military music and a question-mark stroked out, making a sort of illegitimate pound sterling or dollar sign, is titled 'March Cost?', and a love-bird and a glass of champagne is labelled Lady Margaret Sackville.

James Bridie is represented by a knobby potato of bluish cast and truly Irish, ugliness surmounted by an opera hat at a rakish angle; William Jeffrey is objectified by a cogwheel wreathed with 'baby's breath' flowers on a blue satin base; and Willa Muir's 'personality portrait' is a bit of tapestry laid on a torn newspaper, beside red flowers with frilled petals and a plain mousetrap. "Self-improvement, yes," deduced one spectator, "but why the mousetrap?" The reply is: "Intensity, determination and energy. But it does make bonds. Such persons invariably find themselves prisoners of the very things they have created." The case takes the form of an enlarged keyhole.

William Soutar is an electric light bulb resting on a bed of slightly wilted violets. Nearby are three steel nails.

Lewis Spence is a small York ham in marzipan, with magical symbols piped on it in black and green sugar, surrounded by a frayed India-rubber collar.

A J Cronin is a telegraph pole and a bit of billiard chalk and William Power is an assortment of small keys hanging with a pocket corkscrew from a steel ring in the centre of which a portly grey moth is impaled.

Daniel MacDougall is a potato into which a lot of old safety-razor blades have been sunk.

And an opened tin of sardines in a smoke-discoloured lamp globe is labelled (after the well-known Glasgow novel, *No Mean City*) 'No Meaning City'.

My 'reserve bode' for the whole collection is 6 ½d.

NLS MS 27065 ff 50-1

Blossom, *William Johnstone – Mainhill Gallery, Jedburgh*

Rain in Ettrick *(1968), W J – Private Collection*

Raymond Vettese

Bitter Waves

The cauld North Sea,
its bleak horizon,
has aye been at oor side and the gows'
cries and the tinge o brine on air
and the sense o the tides and the waves' rush:
the kennnin o that presence washes throu
every moment, crumbles the dunes, assaults
whit we held aince to be solid.

We live wi the sea, nae as fisher-fowk
afloat on it, heftin siller fae it,
but as fowk wha canna ignore it
even tho we look inland til the reid fields
and the hairst's gowd. The dairk sea's there
(as constant – mair constant – as the seasons)
heaving its waves and the shells and the dross.

Ae day, I think, we'll be ayont
the cauld North Sea, its bleak horizon,
and then we'll ken the ither side
which will only be the sea seen
frae anither angle, frae somewhar else:
it will aye be there, alang wi the gows,
the shells, the tides, the dross, the desire

tae ken whit the horizon mairks
and syne tae ken it's never there,
it's only the sea, brimmed for a moment
in a wee-bit mind that spiers for aye
o boonds, o freedom, but laistly hears
the cauld souch o the bitter waves
that brak even the teuchest shell.

Among Thistles

Thirty years I've been here.
Does it fit yet, my face?
May I now be admitted
a member of the race?

Or am I still too *fremmit?*
Is my tongue still too strange?
Am I still too exotic?
How much more must I change?

Phantoms o Grace

Bricht een that aince dumfoonert,
snared me glaiket as onie ribbit
beglammert by heidlichts.
I didna care then gin mishanter thunnert
wi a juggernaut's wecht o crushin wheels
as lang as your een were on it.

Hoo monie seasons or sic things are safe,
can be written o an' dinna steir up
aa the daftness aince mair? I amna shair.
Ten years gane yet your een are bricht,
ghaist the nicht like stars that sheen nae mair
tho they seem there, skimmerin throu the dairk,
phantoms o grace that winna dee til sicht
for ages yet, for lifetimes on lifetimes.

Bricht een, deid stars, rare beauty tint,
but a span 'yont the tellin haunts the brevity o love.

"MONSTER CATCH" *(Headline)*

Puir cratur,
ye werena daen onie hairm
juist whit ye were meant for
but here ye are,
deid and frozen.
Wrang place at the wrang time
I suppose
but hoo we kill and rejoice
(is that whit we're meant for?)
smile for the photograph,
a grin for death.

Chain

Whit were we then?
Freemen? Slaves?

I think o the lang chain,
generations o graves.

Ach, whit dis it maitter?
We're here noo
and wi nae bairns.
Death is death,
cauld, bare, true.

For us the chain is broken.
Whit we are, whit we were,
snaw aff a dyke,
naethin mair.

Gagool

She craikit, an ancient cratur;
sic a little box for sic a big man,
wha nae doot had said this monies a time
as generations withert again and again.

It wis a wee box. In bricht-alive days
he micht hae stored valuables in it,
a keepsake or twa. Ay weel, stour he wis;
intil whit sma space oor flesh can fit.

The perfunctory meenister got the business ower –
well-known – bla – fine husband – bla –
and we scrunched oot, the graivel crunched dour,
embarrassed oor lugs, and then like a craw

bead-eened on decay, she saw and she kent
I wis the richt ane for sic a feast;
I mind, she haskit, *whan the first ane went.
He wis big tae. Och the big dinna laist.*

And aff she hirpelt, Gagool o Montrose,
a shauchlin, dwinnilt, runkelt survivor,
a joyous crone wha exults as ane dees,
nods and kekkles, driech-shair o forever.

I think o her affen, o whit she meant,
but in truth I confess I amna shair.
Ae day I'll be deid, that I d'a resent;
whit fashes me whiles is kennin she'll be there.

F'ae the Hairt

Quickened by love he sang f'ae the hairt
the beauty o things, hoo nocht wis apairt.

Dairkened by loss he believed this nae mair;
he laboured to grave the truth o despair.

Years by he saw the richtness o baith
but that wis a sang he couldna gie breath

except in the simplest and wycest o words:
Poetry, he said, *that's for the birds.*

Routh

Yon field o ferlies gied us the graith
for biggin oor castles, riggin oor ships,
frae the boxes, prams, tyres – whitna trophies –
fowk dumped here, on The Plots, weel-kept
grund aince but let rin tae seed, forgotten
save by us wha kent whit that freedom meant,
wha raikit amang the weeds, the golochs,
wha shot each ither wi staccato voice
but never deed, rose wi a touch,
alive an whoopin an' ready for mair.

Yon acre wis tarred. Lorries hulk on it.
Yet whiles, in spite o yirdin bleck,
a shoot progs throu, some raggit nail
that points til then, hotchin wi life.
But the routh lies alow us, truly deid,
tho we skart for whit wis or oor fingers bleed.

Message in a Bottle

There wis a bottle
wi layers and layers o sand,
each layer a different colour.
Whan I wis a bairn
yon beguiled me.
It stood on a shelf
ahent the window o a hoose
and I stood and I gawped.

Layers and layers o sand,
each layer a different colour.
Lang syne this wis
yet still I see it,
think o it,
and spier whit held me,
whit hauds me yet,
whit roots yon sae deep

as gin there were indeed
a message in the bottle,
something tae be understood,
tho no by thocht
but by some ither pairt o me.
Layers and layers o sand,
ilka layer a different colour,
layers and layers o sand.

Meg Bateman

Leòmhann

Choimhead sinn a' chèile tron chèids,
tro na h-aon sùilean staoine,
an leòmhann na sìneadh le cuileanan
gun spreigeadh na ruaige,
is mise aig an t-sutha lem chuilean-sa,
is feasgar glas ri lìonadh,
an leòmhann cho fada bho ghrian Afraga
's a bha mise bho spreigeadh na toile.

Lioness

We looked at each other through the bars,
through the same empty eyes,
the lioness listless by her cubs,
lacking the incitement of the hunt,
and me at the zoo with my cub
with a grey afternoon to fill,
the lion as far from the African sun
as I was from the incitement of desire.

Dadaidh

Shaoilinn gum b' fhasa do bhàs
na an caochladh mall seo
a thìodhlaic thu beò an duin' eile;
gum b' fhasa loch de dheòir a shileadh air d' uaigh
na bhith coimhead mo chuimhne a' lobhadh

air fuamhair an aigheir,
le lasadh fhiaclan is cuailein dubha,
a lìonadh làithean m' òige le còmhradh,
a choisrigeadh an saoghal an aran ag èirigh,
an searragan pinc' a ghlacadh fàileadh an t-samhraidh.

Cha shealladh ach an cù ort
beathach beannaicht', mar a sheall sinne,
nach cuireadh ceist, nach dèanadh coimeas,
's e gu h-uasal a' feitheamh ri d' òrdugh,
gu h-uasal gad leantail gu ruig an deireadh.

Cò chunnaic thu
nuair a sheachnainn nad bhreisleach bhaoth thu
no nuair a chromainn thairis air an leabaidh ghroid

gus suathadh nad mhaol àrd fàsail?
Nighean air liathadh a b'eòl dhut

      bho chionn fichead bliadhna
mus deach ar creachadh,
mus deach ar mallachd, ar leinn,
mus deach tuigse a dhùsgadh annainn mean air mhean
airson na bòidhchid a dh'ionnsaicheas bròn.

Daddy

      I thought your death
would be easier to bear than this slow change
that has buried you alive in another man;
easier to weep a loch on your grave
than to watch my picture rot

      of a giant of joy
with flashing teeth and curls of black,
who filled all my young days with talk,
made the world marvellous in rising bread,
in gurgling demijohns trapped summer's scents.

      Only your dog, blessed beast,
looked to you as we did once,
did not question, did not compare,
was proud to wait on your command,
proud to fall in with your plans to his last.

      Who did you see
when I avoided your unstoppable, stupid rant,
or when I'd lean across the stinking bed
to kiss your desolate brow?
A woman grown grey that once you knew

      and twenty years ago knew you
before we were stripped,
before we were cursed, it seemed,
before there wakened in us
the beauty taught by grief.

Toileachas

Do Niall a thug an smuain seachad

'S tric a chunnaic mi iad tighinn ri chèile,
dithis seann eòlach, dithis chroitearan,
is as dèidh dhaibh an latha a bheannachadh
seasaidh iad còmhla gun fhacal tuilleadh,

taobh ri taobh, chan ann aghaidh ri aghaidh,
is iad a' coimhead a-mach air an talamh
a chumas na fhilltean an uile cuimhne,
a' tarraing anail is cùbhraidheachd
tombaca, fuaradh is spùt nan uan,
's an t-eòlas ac' gun cuireadh cainnt
bacadh air a' chomanachadh òrbhuidh ud,
gum briseadh i a-staigh air am mothachadh
air na th' ann de dhualchas eatarra.

Commissioned by BBC Scotland, for National Poetry Day 9th October 2002

Happiness
For Neil who gave the idea

Often have I seen them come together,
two old friends, two crofters,
who after a brief murmured greeting
will stand wordlessly together,
side by side, not facing each other,
and look out on the land whose
ways and memories unite them,
breathe in the air, and the scent of
tobacco and damp and lamb scour,
in the certain knowledge that talk
would hamper that expansive communion,
break in on their golden awareness
of all there is between them.

Jamie Reid Baxter
Antoine de la Roche-Chandieu (translation)
Warldis Bewtie

Warldis bewtie dwynis aye,
Lyk til the wind, it winna stey,
Lyk til the fleur sends furth its scent
And is als sune til yird dounbent,
Lyk til the swaws on ocean's face
That skairss ar cum, bot onwerts race:
Quhatna treuth dois aa thir schaw?
Warld is wind, is fleur and swaw.

(fra Antoine de la Roche-Chandieu (1534-1591), Octonaires de la Vanité du Monde, tr. Martin Opitz (1591-1639))

With Tormad

Ian Stephen

A very wide window. A tray with cold coffee cups sits on its wide ledge. The tomato plants have had it. I think they were tomatoes. One of the spars that looked as if it retained the glass, starts to move as a fishing boat leaves its Bayhead berth. Somewhere in these casements, weights will swing on fraying cordage. Maybe cast in Bonnybridge, between batches of locomotives, stoves and phone-boxes.

People outside pass rapidly. I know some of them. So does Tormad. Even if you've been away longer than you've been home, they stop you in the street and ask what you're up to. It's good. It's social. See after the newness wears off, the big streets of New Zealand or New York, you're looking for a face that recognises you or knew your mother.

But now, no, you've got to stay for a while, give the place a chance. You'll have the downs anywhere, let's be honest, if you're like him and can hardly let go of a dream of settlement. Main streets or back woods, you couldn't help hoping for a log-cabin. Maybe in a tenement.

Of course it falls in about you. Shaky foundation. Better to know it sooner. Bit of bitterness in the wind that blows. No shelter for the time being but you can't be daft enough to go sailing off in search of another South Sea Island where no other bastard from the more desolate parts of the globe has berthed. Anyway commerce goes on. So does work, for the lucky ones. And yourself?

I was working my way back into the town. Intermittently wanting to be a part in its pulse. Travelled a little before, hoped to do so again. Always returning here. If we were seriously interested in the historical aspects of the town we should go and have a look at the Opera House. Maybe I was too young to have swilled hot whisky and cold beer here, down the neck and then pissed it all against the wall. A bit of his life pissing against walls. A good example of a cliché surviving because it's accurate.

We walk to the end of the pedestrian precinct then risk a route across. Ignoring the indicators of fast Fords. Escorts now. They used to be Cortinas. Cairo is the only other town where they drive like this. I've never been there but I've driven with someone who has. And in Cuba they keep the wide and long Oldsmobils and Chevrolets on the road because they have nothing to replace them with, their wings shiny as in the days when Kennedys were Knights.

I watched a moon-landing in this town, no, not a moon descending on the town. Hell you know what I mean, Tormad. Squeezed it in between cycling back from Holm, me and my mate, Kenny, with tails of mackerel, haddock and flounder beating a song in our spokes. Staying with my uncle and auntie for the summer. They let me watch BBC2. Some guy got Pink Floyd to do some space-age music which was still termed Underground in those far-off days. No wonder so many people's grannies still believed the whole thing was set up in a studio in London or Cape Kennedy. We were all talking about how crazy it was with Biafra going on and then we all shut up when the footage happened. That still from Glen's Hasselblad.

Three days after the moonwalk? Splashdown. And that was the day Senator Edward walked, on this earth, away from a drowning car sinking into Chappaquiddick. Mary Jo sank with it. Put to the democratic-ish test, he was re-affirmed as the candidate. He won and his majority was only slightly down on 64. The power of myth but the big dream of the dynasty was all over. Hell of a story to tell me when we're trying to cross a road. Any road. But hell, this road? Who needs to go on the booze?

We're just wandering, Tormad and me. That's what we say round here, you know, so and so and me. All these years, all these teachers, good ones among them, and they never quite got me out of it.

One of the best of all was in the Clock School. Heated up the milk for those that wanted it warm, by the coal fire. Frostiest time of the Cold War. Of course, we guys were all Uri Gargarins. We took it cold.

The Opera House is still standing but only just, near Number Two Pier, across from the Weighbridge. A stink from the joined forces of whisky and ammonia still hangs in the air around it. There is a stout wooden barrier bolted across the entrance. The Opera House is OUT OF ORDER.

See that gate, Tormad says. It would keep a herd of bloody elephants at bay. But it's not enough. There has to be that sign as well. It says a lot, that KEEP OUT.

We go to the café. We've all been banned from these in our day. They've all changed their names, their owners, even if other people's memories are as long as ours. Do you think other people's memories are more forgiving? Do you think they should be?

The seat's got to be where you can look out, see who's going by. And breakfast is important, no doubt about it. You flirt with Muesli, revert to oatmeal porridge, not the flakes. But eggs are probably best. Two of them. Poached ones are all right but fried ones are better. Macbrayne's still do good ones though the slanders about their dinners are not without reason.

You soon get to know the right cafés for breakfasts in all the cities you're liable to find yourself in. Last time it was a London setting. Modest residence in Gypsy something or other road. Was that address appropriate? Or another irrelevance pretending significance. And maybe you chose a flat for all sorts of reasons, including the connotations of its address.

She appeared on the Island. Never met her before. We left together on the Skye ferry. Better route. From it we saw a billow of smoke on the shore. Burning smell mingling with that of the seaweed. Some small flames. A fisherman burning his boat. He too must have been ready for profound change. A poem.

No, it hadn't been long, half a year rather than a full turn of the dial. Of course there was pain when she went back to the States. But no bitterness this time. Ready for home, with a bag of playscripts and a couple of firm offers. Fruitful time, taken in balance.

Back for spring. That's why the telephone's a handy instrument. It alerts a helper to come out on the right day for a long peatbank. One to cut and one to throw. It was great, swinging them to fall with an inch between each one and delicate thuds sounding out to say they were mostly landing fine.

As for the cutting, I hadn't done too bad once I started getting the iron closer in, flush to the wall of the bank. I must have had an earlier teacher. Or else it was genetic. No disrespect but you could always recognise an incomer's peatbank. Unless they'd teamed up with the right squad. Funny until a sheep drowned in it. You're making a new edge, for next year, as you go along. And the village inspection committee would be studying what we'd done. So we shouldn't be too proud to adopt some kind of pride. And then we'd strolled over to that loch, the deep one over the ridge. Tormad said that stories come from it like vapours. Maybe the last water-horse was still down there.

In Tong village, the word was a Heinkel had gone over. Hadn't found a target out the Atlantic and had to drop its heavy load somewhere if it was going to get back. Someone heard the controlled thunder of engines, the loose whine of a falling weapon. Then a delay. Only the engines fading distant. No explosion. They'd gone out next day and hunted the moor. They'd want to find it sooner rather than later, not hit it with an iron, at the peats. Not a trace. No new mud. No visible holes in the wet coat of the Lewis moor.

But all eyes went to that wee deep loch. If there wasn't a sign of it anywhere else, it might be there still.

For Gerry and Morven

East Banks, Shiants, springs, slack water to first hour of flood, wind S to SW 3 to 4

Grey ones curling, whitening at their own low tops,
fulmar fleck, breaking out to the banks.
Bulging now, deep bulk forced shallow –
watch the pulse of these ones.
When shelving disrupts them
they're none too quiet.
We've heard their like before.

Sound of Taransay Low Water Springs, Wind SW to W 4 to 5

Tide's fallen, kick in the arse off the datum.
Breeze is out on her own, a gannet stab at it.
Better that way, salt cream on reefs and stacks,
necks and backs arched in the bit of sun.
The spit is hissing, a temperate lizard
crouching out to the green stuff.
Navigable way, that bit narrower.
Sharper turns than the last time.

Hugh MacDiarmid

The Victory of Patriotism

And this, O Patriotism, is your victory
And this, O Militarism, your goal.
Prove them gallant soldiers, but additional chips
In the seething fire of ambition; feed
The upward leaping flames that glorify
The faces of the brainless great; the greed
Of the degenerates who rule – crazy lunatics
Who forget the common clay from which they spring
And arrogate Divine qualities to themselves: and fling
Better men than themselves to the slobbering
Dogs of war in their drunken frolics.
Their ideas are spawned in idiocy
And fed on alcohol.   *NLS MS 27032 f 106*

In the Blackest Night at Sea

And when in the blackest night at sea I fare
I ken a's weel wi' my soul
Gin I can see the light on the Point of Ayre
Answer the fer-aff gleam on the Mull of Galloway

              And can say
On my left in the dark lies Ireland
Scotland on my right owre there
And, straight aheid, bydand, Norway and the North Pole.
                                   NLS MS 27031 f 29r

Bonus

In the Slums of Glasgow

How many notice, I wonder, even on these grim walls
The little touches the builders made which show
Their easy command of their materials and tools
– The work that into craftsmanship must needs overflow!

The rapid almost dancing movements every here and there,
The little graceful ornaments of action, look, like these
Half-unconscious flourishes of a trowel, delicate *fioriture*
Of consummate dexterity, done with effortless ease.

These slum-folk's lives are full of similar touches too
Even in the unsightliest and most debased of them,
And there are few delights in all the world, I think,
Like chancing now and then on such a gem!   *NLS ACC 12074/9*

Head of Poet, *William Johnstone*
lithograph courtesy of Alan Riach

A Few Head Men after the Deluge

How I would love to be in Glasgow when the storm is over
And see the bits of wreckage – the left-overs of the present sway –
Organically part of the city; kinds of living caryatids,
For a time in a sort of anabiosis frozen away,
Gradually emerging as the city they once controlled reorganises.
But how? That's what I'd like to see – to see them come crawling out;
Our inner struggle against the involuntary impulse for revenge
Successful, I'd like to see a few of these familiar figures about
And our new regime utilising as best it may
Their old experience and skill in the light of a different day
I think I could name all those I would like to see survive
– Or rather begin to live; so far they've been but half-alive.

The greater vengeance will be to quell the impulse for revenge
And let them feel the indomitable will, boldness, & enthusiasm rife
In the changed order; make these proud specialists see
The wise nobility of the simple workers; inspire them
To make good – or try to – in this new life.   *NLS MS 27031 f 151r+v*

The Communist Discipline

You think that life in the Soviet Union
Is a far more terrible tyranny
Than any in any capitalist country?
I do not agree (although it is true
That the cure must sometimes be worse
Than the disease, save for the fact
That the latter is tending to death all the time
And the other to life) – but even if it were,
Consider, life under monopoly capitalism
Becomes more and more for the masses like
Being in a compressor chamber and having
A pressure of something over two atmospheres
Built up – and then suddenly allowed to drop
Back to normal, a treatment
That carbonises the blood and literally turns
The victims into human soda-water bottles.
Most of the seventy-eight per cent of nitrogen in the air
Is ordinarily exhaled, but, under pressure,
Much of it passes into solution
In the bloodstream. If the external pressure
Is reduced gradually the lungs have time
To filter the gas out again: but
If the drop is too rapid the nitrogen returns
To a gaseous state wherever it happens to be

And forms bubbles in the bloodstream and tissues.
Same as when you take the cap off a soda-water bottle.
The bubbles rupture the blood vessels, tear the tissues,
And shatter the nerves: and you've a sure case
Of either road-hog's itch, the staggers, the chokes or the bends
– In other words, the very things from which nearly everyone
In the world under capitalism is suffering today.
But if one can get out from under that pressure
In time – is there, you ask, any cure?
Sure. Recompression. Get back
Into the compressor chamber and back
Under the original pressure – then reduce it
Slowly enough so the gases can escape
Normally through the lungs – do you understand
The meaning of Communist discipline now   *NLS MS 27105 ff 16-17*

Clouds of Glory

If trailing clouds of glory we came
From Heaven and go back there rent of us at death
Isn't it a dreadful waste of time
That we ever had to draw earthly breath.

Isn't it a pity that people couldn't live
In Arcadian innocence all the time
Instead of being jammed in horrible cities
Plague-spots of ugliness, noise and grime.

This is the old illusion – the libel against life –
Of those who think childhood's days are best
– And thereby only show how poorly
They have stood the world's great test.   *NLS MS 27095 f 5r*

Thrilling the Golf Crowds

If there is one shot that thrills golf crowds
More than any other it is the recovery shot
From a greenside bunker that leaves the ball
Nestling at the holeside – not any bunker shot
But only the one where the ball is cut out of the sand
And falls squirming on the green.
The swing should be upright and outside the line of flight,
With the left hand in control throughout.
But the hit must not be stopped at or in the sand.
The clubhead must carry on through the sand and under the ball
Which is squeezed against a coating of sand
On the clubface – the friction set up
Produces the back and side spin

That pulls the ball up sharply,
In other words, cuts the feet from the ball
In almost precisely the manner one executes
A high stopping pitch over a hazard.
– My poetry must have many such cut shots. *NLS MS 27032 f 174*

In Memoriam: John Maclean
(Died, November 30, 1923)

If a stone were let into that grim grey front
Inscribed: 'To the memory of John MacLean',
The whole hideous building would at once fall away
And John walk out a free man again.

If neon lights set up over Glasgow spelt out
'The City for which MacLean gave his life'
– But everybody whispers it, or pretends to forget,
While underneath, underneath – like a bad conscience it's rife.

Underneath, underneath. But it'll win up yet
No matter how careful the cowards may be,
Till the name of the murdered man shines out like his smile
And Glasgow basks in its brave humanity!   *NLS MS 27029 f 14*

Intrinsic Worth

The intrinsic worth of these people you say
Is not what matters here. What they symbolise
Is the important thing. And the rich robes,
The diadems, swords, medals, ribbons
Carry a stupendous significance even tho'
The people themselves are worthless creatures
Not one of them can contribute anything
To the spiritual heritage of humankind.
– I don't agree with you. The fact remains
Shit's shit no matter how it's dressed up. *NLS MS 27031 f 121r*

To Deaf Landlubbers

Let landlubbers wha hae never heard
The unearthly singin note that accompanies
A ship across deep waters, thin, sweet,
Continuous like the music o' a horn, and gies
A celestial accompaniment to the soonds
Made by the ship hersel' as she thrusts
Her timbers, her sheets, and her canvas
Against the waters' wecht and the wind's gusts
Ignore my poetry
On its greater sea.   *NLS MS27032 f 147*

The Sergeant and Two Constables

The sergeant and the two constables
Corroborated each other.
There was no other evidence
And the man in the dock
Protesting his innocence
Was convicted and sentenced.
It happens every day
And I thought to myself
If I were a judge I'd never
Convict on police evidence alone
And as I looked at the three policemen
Shining with self-righteousness now
They had won their case
An old saying ran through my head
– *Once a copper, never a man.*

In the next case a policeman denied
He had beaten a prisoner up in the cell.
True the prisoner was badly bruised
But that must have happened
Before he was arrested, he must
Have fallen while he was drunk
Or got into a fight. And the magistrate
Said the police were a splendid body of men.
He would never believe them guilty
Of any of the brutalities alleged against them
By men like the prisoner
And I remembered two things I'd thought before

It happens every day
And *Once a copper, never a man*   *NLS MS27032 f 220*

The Shifting Shadow

Come doon, eagle, come doon, sun,
Licht upon my shekel-bane
Teach me hoo to gar the black
Shaddaws frae my sang begane.

Flee back, eagle; flee back, sun
For there's naethin' you can tell.
A' my woes are human anes
That [I] maun solve myself.

When we're heich and clear as you
Wha's woes were owre or oors begun
What at least as greater still
'll tyauve wi' shaddaws, eagle, sun?   *Uni of Delaware MS224*

Three People ...

Three people are said to have come back from the dead
But for aught they afterwards did or said
Might better have stayed under a coffin lid
For deeper than in any grave their resurrected lives hid

Nobody knows what happened to the three
Lazarus, Jairus's daughter, and the son of Nain
They were dead and buried and came alive again
Only to vanish as if they had risen in vain.

Surely nothing is stranger. Men have always sought
To plumb Death's mystery but these three brought
None of the knowledge they surely ought
To solve this endless problem of thought

Nowadays of course they'd be front page news,
The subjects of sensational interviews
Try as they might they couldn't refuse
To pay hun curiosity its natural dues.

Was there more privacy in these old days?
Journalism no doubt has changed its ways
But there was many a journalistic ace
Among the New Testament symposiasts to amaze
Us that thus the scoop of all time
– All time and Eternity – was reckoned not worth a dime
And the three who returned from the dead
Only got utter obscurity and silence instead

In these primitive days perhaps it was just
Trifling incidents like these were not discussed
Certainly nobody agitated, nobody fussed.   *NLS MS27031 f 117r + v*

The Poetry I Seek

This is the poetry I always sought for,
Encyclopaedic in its range.
One does not know which to admire most,
The sweep of its generalisations,
Or its vast accumulation of precise detail,
Which is never allowed to clog
The flow, the curve, of the whole.
The loose and gratuitous effects
Of syllabic music no longer used
To prop up the mood. Most of the power
Visual, a close reference to the objects themselves,
The data of emotion strictly conveyed,
A poetry that starts at the level of gossip,

Of conversation, of news,
Of the object seen and heard.
That much always scrupulously given
What is added is a heightening of perception,
A formal arrangement which throws the words into relief,
A perspective of evaluation,
A swift and ruthless development,
My fingers firm on the core of the poem
– Scotland in the hollow of my hand.   *NLS MS27032 f 14r+v*

Unstable as Water

The unstable as water alone can excel.
Instability, like drink, is one of the solvents of life.
It has nothing inherently evil in it,
Nor anything inherently good.
It does a lot of damage
To men's brains and bodies;
But it does less damage in sum,
From the eternal standpoint,
Than drab duty-people who are always
Wearisomely doing right. Oh, much less!
Running water may go to waste,
May even tear out a few bridges;
But stagnant water breeds pestilence.   *NLS MS27105 f 32*

Conferences with the Dead

O that it were possible we might
But hold some two days' conferences with the dead!
From them I should learn something I am sure
I never shall learn here.   *NLS MS27092 f 54*

Somerset Maugham

Somerset Maugham once wrote a story
About a Scotsman, manager of an estate
Sixty miles from Seville. Just beyond
The boundary of the estate was a ruined cottage
Where, twenty years previously, a madman had died.
On the night of the full moon the Scotsman
Began to hear the madman's screaming laughter.
This happened every month. At last
He could stand it no longer & returned to Seville.
On the first night of the full moon
He heard it again, and knew then
He would never be able to escape

From that fiendish laughter for the rest of his life
I feel very much the same about all
I have said, or read. It pervades & hauants my life   *NLS MS27025 f 31*

The Gulf of Silence

There's little expression in their faces
And when you look at them
A shadow may seem to flick fleetingly
Across your ain, and you can feel
A gulf o' silence risin' atween you
– A silence that only comes
When folk canna explain their way o' life,
Even if they're misunderstood
Because o' that silence.   *NLS MS27137 f 9*

Poets as Canaries

Since poets are the canaries whose silence means
The presence of noxious gases in the atmosphere
It is not surprising there has never been
A poet of any worth in Glasgow here.   *NLS MS27031 f 161r*

Winning the Final Form

Say of me, 'He never forgot the breed he belonged to
And therefore was content through all adversity
Foreknowing how at last with him it would be
As with a Mountain Shape that comes through
Several glacial epochs and periods of maximum pressure
Of destructive forces, with a measure
Of more genial but still strenuous interludes no doubt
Till, amid the collapse of similar peaks, it stands out
(As he does now) its final form won,
Slightly battered, a shade forbidding in bleak weather
In its tattered garb of old heather
But amply responsive to the sun.'   *NLS MS27122 f 10v*

After Inverurie

Only one occasion
Would I have loved to witness – after Inverurie (1745)
When Lord Louis Gordon's pipers kept silence
Since Duncan Ban MacIntyre was his prisoner
No Scottish Army or English, no army in the world
Would do that today – nor ever again –
For they do not know and there is no means of telling them
That Kings and Generals are only shadows of time

But time has no dominion over genius
The silent bagpipes of Lord Louis Gordon
On the morning after the battle of Inverurie
Was the greatest tribute ever paid to genius. *NLS MS27032 f 74r*

Translation of 'The Heron' by Sorley MacLean

A pale, yellow moon on the skyline
The heart o' the soil deid to lauchter
A daithlikeness thrawin' contempt
On gowden windas in a sea that moves like a snake!

It's no the frail beauty o' the moon
Nor the cauld gracefulness o' the sea
Nor the irrelevant noise o' the beach's uproar
That seeps through my spirit to-night.   MS27126 f.31v

Land D'ye Think?

Is it land d'ye think or juist a line
O' the grey sea heavin' there?
Europe you say, but you're aiblins wrang
And in ony case why should I care?

Nae doot if I could see far eneuch
Lookin' west I'd see anither sic line
– that micht be America – but I'll no' fash
To rax my een. I'm glad it's hyne.   MS27138 f.39r, 1956-7

Returning to Scotland

When I return to Scotland I shall be
Like one who used to live the circling year
And knew it stage by stage but this year comes
When Summer like its shadow must appear

He knows what he has missed of all he loved;
The beauties bloomed as usual – not for him;
It seems incredible such great fires flamed
Without his presence and now lie low and linn

When I return to Scotland I shall see
The fallen leafs of all the seeds I cast;
I was the spring; others shall reap; and I
Get only late Autumn & the winter blast   *NLS MS27031 f 164r*

That Wumman

That wumman owre yonder's a widow
A wumman that has been neglected
A wumman slightly bitter about marriage
A wumman seein' the sand o' life, he said

Slippin' through her fingers, in short
A wumman like Scotland ever sin' Flodden
Wi naething to dae but watch
Her mind narrow as her hips broaden   NLS MS 27032 f.199

Mean Faces

Where have I seen this mean face before,
With the wolfishness showing through
The patrician veneer, that gives me
Such a sense of déjà vu?

I know – in these trick Victorian engravings;
A fine smiling face, pleasant yet dull,
Seen in the distance, but brought closer up
Becoming just a horrible empty skull.   *NLS MS27030 f 76*

British Labour & Socialism

British Labour & Socialism like Herodotus' lion
Is still trying it seems – but without avail –
To bring its courage up to the scratch,
By beating its sides with its tail   *NLS MS27032 f 121r*

Clear the Streets of these Monsters

Clear the streets of these monsters – blue boars,
Red lions, black swans – if you will:
Let all that unnatural history go
But leave me at least 'The Open Arms' still   *NLS MS27032 f 167*

Cut-throat Competition

To wade through slaughter to a crown has been
The way of tyrants all the ages down,
But here are folk who do not hesitate
To wade through living death for half a crown.*NLS Acc 12074/ 9*

Hic Jacet

Here lies a Premier of England.
What need to give his name?
Many have held that post; but who
Could name a tenth of them?   *NLS MS27030 f 24*

In Defence of the King

If anybody in my hearing ventures
To question our constitutional monarch's worth
I'm always ready to defend him – as
The greatest ventriloquist's doll on earth!   *NLS MS27030 f 36*

Comrades   Ode to the North Wind

The Goal   The Right End of the Stick

Lithographs by William Johnstone in Poems to Paintings *(Kulgin Duval, 1967)*
(Ronald Wilson, Old Town Bookshop, Edinburgh)

A Curious Bird

I agree with you, of course,
I am a curious bird
But I think you'll agree
Never at a loss for the wrong word.   *NLS MS27032 f 111v*

The Water of Life

We Scots have churned all the seas of the world
For centuries and less Amrita won
Than almost any of our ancestors could distil
Almost any afternoon from the Minch alone.   *NLS MS27031 f 28r*

What Cause Hae I to Sing

You spier me, what cause hae I to sing
Seein' I've got naewhaur yet?
Dod! mules aye whinny on reachin' camp,
Horses on leavin' it.   *NLS MS27105 f 21v 1941*

It Was Wild Fishing

It was wild fishing. The stream – except in a few parts cleared along the
bank for meadow, was closely edged by backlash-catching wood & an
undergrowth of wild roses etc. It was an ice-cold stream of great variety.
Wide shallow ripples would end in long still pools. Then the stream
narrowed and deep rapids would swirl through broken banks & suck into
deep whirlpools. It was there the Kings of Stream lived & lorded it. The
old sinners were wise and wary – I caught one with a moustache of
feathered hooks from bygone battles still fastened in his upper lip. Lying
out only our heads peeping over the bank feed the trout on grasshoppers
& bugs, our rod forgotten, for the sheer joy of watching the rush, the swirl
and the strike.   *NLS MS27034 f 110r*

A Great Wall of Weather-painted Granite

A great wall of weather-painted granite, topped by a chain of grass-
covered hillocks, that ended in a dominant green-capped knoll. Slopes and
shallow cups of land, dipping towards the edge of the precipice, make an
undulant, irregular line, and at the landward end one declivity, scarred by
a path, comes down almost to the beach of the cove. The grim wall of the
headland was rooted in water; its base, like its top, was a broken line,
though here, in contrast to the alleviating note of grassy planes and curves,
there was and accent of harshness in tumbled jagged rocks. Spray spun
high, and the water of the cove heaved and subsided under a shifting lace-
work of foam. The rain-wet turf shone richly. The sun found lights of ochre
and red and coppery green in the dark browns and purple blacks on the
cliff's sheer face. Out from the land reached that freckled, mottled wall,

and the foot of it was veiled with spume and dressed in frilly skirts of white water. Gulls wheeled and hovered, swooped, paused in air, and floated down like snowflakes against the black background of rock. Their screams, high-pitched, intense, cut through the low note of surf – Peering steadily out across the wind-curdled sea – In the changing light under voyaging clouds – A dull speck of sail shone for a moment or two, a small fore- and-after with a brown rag of foresail etc. And a reefed mainsail – a French crabber no doubt – becomes 'lines' of poetry *NLS MS27097 f 51r+v*

Sound Was Frozen

Sound was frozen – come a thaw all the incessant tiny noises of nature would dissolve and produce a wild bedlam of rustles, squeaks, ripples, drips, rumbles & whispers.

Spring is brief – May flowers are delivered by some miracle. The starlings come in iridescent clouds. The brilliant wood-duck chuckles to his mate in the eddies of the flooding stream. Horses, cattle, men, snakes all shed their winter coats. It's all a headlong business.

An endless clamour of things long frozen fetching loose, dead branches, freed from the winter's rigor mortis, being torn off by wind. The drain gurgled and chuckled and whispered with delight.   *NLS MS27034 f 109r*

Note: The above poems and prose fragments are not *included in* The Revolutionary Art of the Future, Rediscovered Poems by Hugh MacDiarmid, *disinterred mainly from the National Library of Scotland archives by John Manson and published last October by Carcanet (£6.95), to which volume I heartily recommend readers.*

Cartoon by Gerald Mangan

Disney Exist

Alastair Sim

It should have occurred to him earlier. It should not have taken a man with an MBA from the Texas Agricultural and Mechanical University nearly a year to work out how to run a theme park in Coatbridge.

Elmore looked out from his office in the highest tower of Cinderella's Fairy Tale Castle. Below him, huddled figures trudged grimly through the rain from attraction to attraction. A mother was skelping a child outside the Baloo Bear Hug-Hut. The round black fibreglass ears that marked the park's location from a distance were swaying in the wind.

Elmore had had his doubts from the start. When he'd been assigned to manage Disneyland Scotland the location had already been chosen and construction work was under way. He'd imagined somewhere like Briga-doon, surrounded by heather clad hills, and had to admit some disap-pointment when he'd seen the site. The economics boys (who, Elmore suspected, had never actually seen the place) had explained that Coat-bridge made perfect sense because there was cheap derelict land, loads of government grants, and three million people within 40 minutes' drive.

His accommodation hadn't been what he'd expected either. The estate agent hired by the Disney Corporation had sent him descriptions of a choice of houses in different parts of Glasgow. They'd been pretty unin-formative – three bedrooms, one public room, located in an up-and-com-ing part of the city – and Elmore had chosen an apartment in Rutherglen because he thought he'd enjoy having a real Scottish glen in his back yard. Since moving he'd had his car broken into twice and had come to seri ously regret that a man wasn't allowed to carry a handgun in this country.

Still, the opening of a new Disney park was a big event in any man's life, and things had got off to a pretty good start. The sun shone on the opening day, the provost of North Lanarkshire had kept her speech about the work-ing man's fight for justice mercifully short, thousands of people had taken advantage of the opening-day offer of free admission, and all the rides worked. You couldn't ask much more of a Disney manager than that.

The problems had only started to emerge after that. Part of it was the competition – Carfin Grotto was putting up a surprisingly strong fight by marketing itself as 'Pope-land' and offering an indulgence to every visitor with the price of entry. But the main problems were internal.

The first thing that Elmore had noticed was that there were always some left-over children in the park at closing time. He'd initially thought that there must be a fair handful of distraught parents getting separated from their offspring, and that he needed to set up some specific place in the park where families could easily meet up, and where lost children would be looked after until they were recovered. The curious thing was that practically none of them ever were recovered, and at the end of each day social services would predictably have to take seven or eight children away. Even when he'd had to put the admission charge up, there were still left-over children every day – the parents must have reckoned that £12 was a fair price to pay for getting rid of their progeny.

The park had had more than its fair share of staff problems too. Elmore had hired a local as Director of Human Resources for the park. In retrospect, McManus had been a poor choice. Elmore hadn't realised that McManus had been handing out different coloured application forms – green for people from Coatbridge and orange for people from Airdrie – or that the orange forms had been going straight in the bin. When the newspapers had pointed this out it had been quite an embarrassment, and Elmore had learnt that people who never went to church could get quite bothered about religion. McManus didn't quite seem to have the Disney work ethic either – Elmore hadn't liked hearing that McManus was briefing the new recruits that "you're allowed ten days self-certificated sick leave a year, so stick that on yer leave entitlement and we'll no ask any questions".

You couldn't really blame McManus for everything. People here just didn't seem to understand service. Across the world, Disney liked to make some acknowledgement of the culture of the country they were in. 'Granny's Highland Howff' was meant to do it for Disneyland Scotland. "Enjoy a traditional Scottish welcome and the finest Highland fare," said the guide. It really was very disappointing to go into the Howff and reliably be told that "the special's aff" and "we dinnae serve lunch after 1.30 – ye should have read the sign on the door, mister". And it was most irritating that the staff insisted on taking their breaks at lunchtime, just when the queues were longest.

What had worried Elmore most was the quality of staff they'd hired to play Disney's well-loved cartoon characters. McManus really ought to take some of the blame for this – it was indisputably insensitive to publicise a nationwide talent competition for midgets to fit into the Huey, Dewey and Louie costumes. After such an intensive competition it was all the more surprising that one of the characters would shout "Huey" at children and then pretend to throw up on them, although most of the kids seemed to find this quite funny for some reason.

Goofy had been just about the worst. To Elmore's horror, it turned out that Mickey and almost all his friends were trade union members, in strict contravention of Disney policy, and that there was nothing he could do about it. Goofy was their shop steward, and you couldn't ask for a more cussed character. He'd already threatened that the whole crew were going to take their costumes and demonstrate outside the Scottish Parliament until Disney paid Equity rates plus 20% 'absurdity allowance'. But it was Goofy's personal behaviour with the visitors which bothered Elmore most. When a child came up and said "Hello Goofy", it really was not satisfactory to say "Piss off, Ah'm on ma lunch break".

In his bleaker moments Elmore had wondered whether there was anything he could do to improve the quality of the visitors themselves. He had made his first mistake when he was walking round in the first week the park was open, just to see how things were going. Even though he was wearing a shirt, tie and slacks a couple of visitors had recognised him as a staff member – the ears must have been the giveaway. "Hey mister," had said a spotty youth holding hands with what Elmore assumed was his younger sister, "can we shag in the Lost Valley Ghost Train ride?" Elmore's British vocabulary had been a bit more limited then, and he'd given what he thought was the most tactful answer. "Sure, you're the guest, you can do whatever you like in Disneyland as long as it doesn't upset our other guests." Word had obviously got around since then that the management let you 'shag' on the rides and it was proving impossible to stamp this out. And it had taken Elmore quite some time to realise that there was a problem with 'jellies' being sold in the Gingerbread House.

It was only when he'd started to think about who the visitors were, and what they wanted, that Elmore realised that things were a lot better than he'd realised. Here he was, on a blustery March day, and over two thousand people were in the park. They were queuing for up to an hour in the rain to get onto the Buzz Lightyear Flight of Terror, queuing again for a Pocahontasburger and fries, they were getting ignored or sworn at by the characters, the little train round the park wasn't working because of industrial action by ASLEF, they were running a pretty high chance of being pickpocketed, and they were loving it. These people were getting exactly what they wanted.

It was an epiphany. Elmore suddenly realised that all the things which he had thought were problems were actually reasons for Disneyland Scotland's success. If you wanted to give Scottish people what they wanted you didn't give them the best quality of service you could, you gave them the mediocrity they were comfortable with and thought they deserved.

Elmore returned to his desk and started to sketch out ideas for Scot-friendly attractions which he could build in the park. Maybe an 'Ochone-zone' where Highlanders would talk endlessly about the Clearances and public subsidy. Or a new maze called 'The Scheme', based on East Kilbride's street plan and where you'd be jumped by actors dressed as muggers if you took a wrong turn. There was a flute band in Shotts that could lead parades down Main Street …

The one remaining problem was the name. 'Disneyland' was just too American and didn't really stand for the quality of experience which the park now offered. But it would be an awful waste of money to get rid of the rides and costumes which the park already owned. There must be a compromise.

Elmore scored out the Disneyland heading from some notepaper, and wrote in his first attempt at a new title for the park.

'Scot-land: come to the Mickey Mouse country'.

Rob MacKenzie

Nuclear Deterrent

The day after three middle-aged women
turned over Trident, lacing its insides
with syrup and bundling its computers into
the Gareloch, I read the morning news.

Magnifying glass in hand, I spied a
column somewhere to the left of page
nine, detailing anonymous arrests.
For some reason this made me hungry.

Passing over my usual cereal breakfast,
I boiled an egg so hard it mimicked the
texture of stone, smouldering like sulphur in
the salty depths, armoured against the stab

of ploughing cutlery, those who wanted
to split the whole shell open. I could do
nothing with it. Walls quivered like jelly,
the rockery switched to india rubber.

I bent a spoon over its head, its blank
face staring like Medusa. One touch and
objects previously concrete became
flaccid and impotent reflections

of themselves, bouncing the egg back
like a bagatelle. I wondered whether it
could be used to soften up Trident.
The local activists' committee warned me to

say nothing. Such tomfoolery, they said,
was bad for morale. As peace campaigns
were executed with military precision, a
stiff upper lip was required at all times.

Eggs, then, being no match for the nuclear
threat, we placed our trust in jumpered vicars
who strained their flimsy dog-collars to the limit,
bulging adam's apples with fruity hymns

set for guitars and fiddles. Even the navy
staff tapped their feet in rhythm, that old-time
religion and its half-remembered ritual on
the point of re-enacting itself, the snip of

wire, the snatch of arrests, and home in
time for Sunday roast; not before I pitched
my egg into the loch, and just as it struck
water, I'm sure it cracked a wicked grin.

Morning Thirst

One too
    many

        sleepless nights
   lips dry

as a sunburned
      corpse,

       three fifteen in
  the morning,

a glass
    of water

       scorched by
  the kitchen

striplight's
    crazed buzz,

       a stroboscopic
  flicker

in the glass
    like a flame,

       its tongue
  licking

the back of
    the throat

       like
  a hot coal.

Illustration by Daniel Plant

Bleak Outpost

On a bleak outpost in Eastern Europe,
grey drizzle and freezing fog host a grim
Cold War. Map in hand, Craig corners
a wooden bench to mark a route home.

A railway station, a name without vowels,
the train thirteen hours late, and nobody's
guessing when it's due. Craig studies
contours, transport hubs, boundaries.

A coal freighter groans past, the wheels of
industry creaking north with an endless load,
and in pursuit, a belch of factory smoke
like an albatross shadow weighs overhead,

until the wind rips apart the illusion of free
flight. Craig vows he will never again go
beyond the armchair religion of the homespun
truth, the folk wisdom of the talk show.

He'll rail at trains and their diminishing
returns, the anonymous towns without pity
which erased his tracks. Forget the girls who
muddled his head in every shuffling city,

left unpaid bills, unused beds, and muffled
laughter in a language he couldn't share.
Forget the empty space on every bench, and
the beautiful strangers who didn't sit there.

He'll judge the world from his bedroom window;
the devil take the swivel of the weather vane.
He'll ride miles in his mind, and never have
to feel again, the fog, the wind, the rain.

Jazz Flower

She is blossoming, flowers in her eyes
the size of treetops. She presents me
with a sky-blue bouquet,

calls me for a tune. I grow dry cacti
in my desert house, but catch
the late night autumn mood,

the need for rain like soft music on
the window, the light drift of petals on
the mantelpiece. My horn.

I blow some old Duke Ellington,
In A Sentimental Mood, all rise
and fall, like her eyes,

every blink a new note that no one has
dreamt a name for, just as the scents
of flowers have no names.

The saxophone scales heights
and depths, where only the bees
had droned before.

Confessions of a Bookworm

Those empty shelves. High time you stacked them,
                top to bottom,

with the childhood fictions that print the hidden truth
                about you closer

than your shadow. Put them on display. They've waited
                too many years,

perfect bound in crates and boxes for a removal van
                that never comes.

I'm all eyes, invisible girl. I'll let you read my forthcoming
                Booker prize flop

for one peek at the uncut mysteries of Nancy Drew,
                and your complete

Famous Five collection, with the cine-film of you camped
on the desert

island at the foot of your garden, imaginary dog in tow,
while crooks knocked

Uncle Quentin's block off. You solved the mystery on
your space hopper,

flattening guilty rose bushes, extracting thorns with pliers
until they confessed.

So start loading. Let's see how much weight the
shelves can take.

Illustration by Daniel Plant

Leaving

Jenni Daiches

My grandmother watched the *Mont Blanc* burning in Halifax harbour. She saw her blow up. Five days later she got on a train and headed west. She didn't know where she was going and she didn't tell anyone she was expecting. She ended up in a place called Gibson's Landing, where she got a job in a bakery.

Grandma raised her daughter on her own, never married again. The child spent her first ten years with the mountains at her back and the sound of the Pacific Ocean in her ears. Then they went to Vancouver, where they could still see the mountains, unless the cloud was low, which it often is, but they didn't hear the ocean any more. Grandma worked at anything she could get, as long as it wasn't too near the docks. Because in her head that was too close to where grandfather was blown up. He was a docker. He must have seen the *Mont Blanc* too, as she slowly headed into harbour. Maybe he saw the other boat, and the collision. They watched the flames as she drifted closer and closer to the dockyards. She was carrying explosives, but of course they didn't know that. Grandma looked for him in all the hospitals and all the places that had been turned into makeshift hospitals. But he had to be dead. There was nothing left of the place he was working.

Ma said that grandma never talked about it until my sister and I were growing up. Then she told us about the explosion, the earth shaking and the sound of breaking glass. She worked in a house that looked out over the harbour. "I was daydreaming," she said, in a voice that always leant on the vowels. "Dreaming of the future. I used to do that in those days. We had such plans." The *Mont Blanc* rounded the breakwater. The window grandma was staring through was shattered – all the front windows were blown out. Grandma had a tiny scar above her left eye where a shard of glass had fixed itself. There were horses in the stable at the back and they screamed and kicked the door down and galloped off down the street, through glass and twisted metal and buckled paving slabs and people milling and crying. Grandma said that when she felt the boom of the explosion she went icy cold. "Everything stopped," she said. "My life froze." Although the ground was heaving. When at last she moved, out of the front door – she'd never gone out of the front door before – and tried to get to the docks, her feet were blocks of lead.

Everywhere was smoking with fire and dust. Pieces of shattered boats were flung onto the shore. Pieces of shattered people. Sheets of flames seemed to have a life of their own, leaping out of nothing. Grandma said she didn't know how long it took her to get to where the docks had been, or even why she went, because how could anyone be still alive? She didn't know how she propelled herself, how she knew where to go, who to ask, in all that chaos, with the smell of burning everywhere. "But I would have known him anywhere," she said, "even if all I found was his little finger." Her English was uncertain then, although she had had to speak it in school. "They spoke Gaelic where grandma came from," Ma said, when we talked about it later. "Imagine struggling with a foreign language in all that shock and panic." I thought of a fog, but with a texture that was gritty and abrasive. I thought of time suspended.

One of the horses was shot because it got in the way of an ambulance and the other was never seen again. Stolen, probably. The woman grandma worked for was inconsolable. When grandma came back after her five-day search she was screamed at, so she left. She and grandfather lived in a rented room and kitchen and didn't have much more than they'd arrived with a year or so earlier. Grandma left his clothes and took only the bible of their few books. She kept a tortoiseshell comb and a brooch that had belonged to her mother, and I still have them. Most of the household stuff she gave to a neighbour. She wrapped herself in a plaid, probably the same one we found folded in a box under her bed after she died.

In the last few months of her life grandma reverted to her native Gaelic. I had never heard her speak it before, or at least not in sentences. But I tried to listen, not so much to the words as the sound. By the time I started school we were living in North Vancouver, grandma, my mother, me and my older sister Rosie. My father had left by then, I don't remember him. Ma had gone to college – that was where they met – and was a teacher. She didn't give it up when she had us, and I don't think he liked that. Not that mother ever said, so I'm just guessing, but Rosie reckons the same. Grandma looked after us while Ma was at work. She lived with us of course, and maybe he didn't like that either. My father's name was Daniel Gunn, and Ma told us he was descended from a Hudson's Bay fur trader and that was why he had itchy feet. His itchy feet took him off, anyway. It seems he went to Hong Kong, but the last we heard he was in Saskatoon.

So Ma was Mrs Gunn but after a while she changed back to her maiden name and always called herself Ellen McNeil, not Miss or Mrs, and it was before the days of Ms. But me and Rosie were Gunns. So there we were the four of us, growing up quite ordinary, even though there wasn't a man in the house, and wouldn't be until Rosie and I started dating and bringing young men home. If Ma had men friends she kept them away from us. Rosie was more restless than me, and cleverer, so when she was eighteen she went to Toronto. I remember when she left on the train. I remember us all in our summer dresses on the platform, Rosie with a full skirt and a wide white leather belt and wearing lipstick. Grandma's hair was white by then, and she always wore heavy shoes so that every step seemed deliberate and purposeful even when she was an old lady. Ma had on a seersucker suit. We all kissed Rosie goodbye and I cried when the train pulled out and the whistle blew.

I stayed in Vancouver. I went to college and, like Ma, qualified as a teacher. I met Lenny. We'd go walking in the mountains, and I was achingly happy. We'd walk and climb, lie in each other's arms on the soft forest floor, nervous, of each other and of bears. There were always noises in the woods. Late in the afternoon we'd come down through the thick cedars and the huge grey rotting stumps with the low sun filtering through, tired, singing 'You are my sunshine', holding hands. After grandma died I began to think about Ma getting old, wondering whether she was happy. Could you be happy without a man, without a husband? How would I feel if she got together with someone? Her beautiful hair was beginning to go grey. She was still teaching, and I know she loved the kids, seven and eight year olds. She'd come home, make dinner, mark books, and in the evenings get on with her patchwork. She'd sit on the old sofa, bought used like most of the stuff in the house, with her feet curled under her and the bright colours of the patchwork spread out around her.

In those days I'd get up on a weekend morning and look out of my bedroom window at the sun on the mountain tops, and I could hardly breathe for how wonderful it all seemed. But sometimes I would start to think, for no particular reason, about my grandfather, blown up in 1916, and my father who walked out in 1946.

It didn't work out with Lenny, and I thought that was it, there would never be anyone else. But I met a man from Prince George. His father worked for the CPR. Stephen was a technical designer. He had a studio apartment in Kitsilano, where he liked to play at being a Bohemian. But it was only play, I could tell. I thought he was safe, solid, not like Lenny. He didn't sing like Lenny but that's not what you look for in a husband, I thought. I don't think Ma cared for him much, although he was always so polite when he came to the house and insisted on doing the dishes and fixing the cellar door, which was slightly warped, and any other odd jobs around the place, and made sure he didn't smoke anything unconventional. So we got married, and a few months later Rosie got married too, and there we were, happy families. About twice a year we all got together, crammed into my mother's house for Christmas and sometimes in the summer, but it seemed strange. The men seemed large, out of place. The rooms were too small.

Looking back, I sometimes think my mother was just waiting for the inevitable. We had kids, of course, two girls each, and maybe equally of course our husbands departed. Rosie's Doug went first, and she called from Toronto to say good riddance. She had a university job by that time, and promotion, and reckoned Doug felt outshone. He took up with his secretary, and then married a dental hygienist. Rosie and I drank a lot of wine one night I was visiting her in Toronto, and laughed our heads off. That was after Stephen had gone too. He shacked up with a woman who had recently joined his firm, an engineering PhD. Rosie stabbed the corkscrew into the second bottle and said, "Jeanie, maybe we should have swapped husbands," and we laughed some more. "What is it with this family?" my mother said, with an unaccustomed steel edge to her voice. "The men just vanish, evaporate." She might have added, "Or get blown up."

Our girls are grown now. I'm proud of mine. Ishbel's got a good job

with a publisher in Montreal and Shonagh is working her way around the
world. They're good-looking girls, too, taller and slimmer than I ever was.
Ishbel has my mother's red hair. Sometimes I think Shonagh has a look
of grandma, whose name she has. Rosie's two are just as clever as their
mother. Ma died suddenly one June afternoon in her garden. She was
found by a young Salish boy who did odd jobs for the neighbours. He
called the ambulance and came on his bike all the way to Kitsilano. "I
didn't want to tell you on the phone," he said. I think her life had been
okay. She'd been weeding, though I kept telling her I would come over
and do it. But she liked to spend time in the garden and I guess she'd have
preferred to go that way, her heart giving out because she was trying too
hard. She was in her eighties.

Not long before we'd been sitting on the back porch with cups of coffee
and doughnuts, a late Sunday morning breakfast, and she'd started to talk
about grandma. She told me that grandma had once said to her, when she
was a little girl, that one day they would go back to Knapdale. I hadn't
ever heard the name before. Ma wasn't sure exactly where it was but I
found a book about the Highlands in the library which showed me. Ma
said it had come back to her all of a sudden, crystal clear, grandma in the
kitchen making scones, talking about the people around the hearth in the
spring of 1914. Her father, a widower, her sister who had brought them
all up, her three brothers. Two would be killed in the war, one at sea. After
grandma left for Nova Scotia, newly wed to Duncan McNeil, her father
gave up the croft and went with her sister to Greenock. Then there was
the war and they got out of touch.

But grandma described them all in the light of the fire as if they were
there in the Gibson's Landing kitchen, and it had seemed to Ma like a
story, the motherless children, the three fine young men, the hard-work-
ing sister. But now she was thinking of it as her family, not a story any
more but history, and I said, "Why don't we go?" Ma smiled, and I thought
how frail she looks, her skin like crushed silk, her fingers trembling a little.
"Yes," she said. "Why don't we go?"

Time ran out. I thought I might ask Ishbel and Shonagh to come with
me, but then I decided, no, I'll go on my own. I've been here a week now,
staying in Mrs Macmillan's bed and breakfast in Cairnbaan. I walk a lot.
I watch the boats pass on the canal. It's September and the weather is much
warmer than I expected. I walk by the canal where the water is tinged pink
by reflected willow herb. I've been up the hillside and found the broken
walls of steadings, and walked among the planted trees, much smaller, less
rich a growth than I'm used to. There's a tiny graveyard where McNeils
are buried. I took off my shoes and dipped my feet in a brown burn. I don't
quite know what I'm looking for, but you never know what might happen.

There are much older stones than the deserted houses, wedges of rock
standing in fields, slabs with strange markings and drawings. There are
places where people met and argued and agreed, sometimes, surely – and
fought. And where children were born. I asked Ma once what my grand-

mother's name had been before she was married, but she shook her head. She didn't know.

So I look at the McNeils in the graveyard, and the other names around them, Campbell, Macmillan … Last night I went up the hill above Crinan and watched the sun set beyond the islands. There were two or three boats, their white sails glinting in the last of the light. My grandfather probably came from one of those islands. He wasn't a Knapdale boy, grandma said, but got casual work on the canal, in the summer when the steamers brought crowds of Glasgow trippers. On my way back I saw a man on the canal bank, staring into the water with his hands shoved in his pockets. He looked up as I came along the towpath, grey hair, about my age. "Grand evening," he said. I nodded and stopped. He didn't look at me, but carried on talking. "I fished a baby in a bin bag out of the canal last week." As I stood beside him I was aware of a chill in the breeze that trickled from the west. We stood side by side, silent for a few moments. "I can't imagine," I said, "I just can't imagine. To be so desperate as to drown your baby." "Aye," he said. "A life over before it's started." "Aye." "Was she a local girl?" "Mebbe. Who knows? If she was, she kept her secret, probably left the area, probably won't come back."

And I walked back to Mrs Macmillan's. Did they come here in their courting days, I wondered, while thinking of a dead baby, a desperate young woman. Did they go up the hill to find a quiet place among the trees? Were they afraid on the boat, slipping down the Clyde with hundreds of others bound for Nova Scotia? Did they think, we will never set eyes on this land again? Dusk was coming gently. There was a smell of fire and falling leaves in the wind now. An explosion, Duncan McNeil was never found. Grandma got on a train and continued the journey. It doesn't end, does it?

Jenni Daiches

Islanders

for Valerie and Dave Siddal

Here sunlight is keen as wind
and rock darkens the water.
Trees lie where gales
have felled them.

True invention is to create
another world regardless,
to raise new space
and animate the old.

Seed potatoes wait
shoulder to shoulder with ivory
and silver. A low roof shelters
ebony and jade.

In this island house we eat
Welsh rarebit from porcelain
and drink Mediterranean
wine from crystal.

More islands spill beyond
the window, the mountains of Mull,
crouching Scarba, the knuckled
hand of Jura.

Seaweed blankets the lazybeds.
The islanders brought their lives
to this place and plant an earth
of alien ancestors.

The dogs escort us to the boat.
The blades dip clean as knives.
When the islanders wave
the ragged shore opens like a door.

Departure

A doubtful, doubled sun disturbs the water.
Our business here is simply pleasure, a walk
by the broad arc of brown canal silvered
by sky and cloud. The green bank is freckled
with snowdrops. A blue boat rests by the bridge
and the tall white house. They astonish, these small things.
They make way as we walk, they allow us to pass, as if
we belong on this imperfect path.

                                    Almost
an island, almost encompassed by canal and white-flecked
loch, the land breathes water. A billow
of wind whips the tide. I see us surrounded,
cut loose, afloat, the house, birch trees, daffodils
not yet out. With moorhen and heron we are swept
wildly south, past the barbed mountains
of Arran, and westward to new Atlantic worlds.

Professor Jameson's Instructions

Today a polar bear arrived, compliments
of Captain Scoresby, trophy of his latest Greenland
whaling. I'm feeding the bear on horse flesh. Generally,
I prefer dead animals, skins and skeletons.
From Africa I crave the pelts of panthers, leopards,
jackals, and the heads of gazelle and antelope.

The bear's in perfect health, lodged at the college
in a commodious den. The captain's kind despatch
of walrus bones is also deeply felt.
Skins can be removed with a blunt knife –
make a straight incision from vent to throat
but leave the skull attached. Preserve fishes
and reptiles in rum or whisky; insects are best
unpacked by the delicate fingers of ladies. I shall write
again to Captain Scoresby, for I yearn for the head
of a sea unicorn and the skins of Greenland birds,
and if I might prevail upon the whalers
to seek out the finny turtle I'd be content.

Study these creatures, my friends. Cross frontiers
with them, like the men on the frozen seas and the hot
savannahs, who trek the mind's interiors without maps.

(Robert Jameson was Professor of Natural History at Edinburgh University, 1804-54)

Robert Campbell of the Hudson's Bay Company Looks for a Wife

Out of the silent trees come the native
people. Their soft buckskin is nothing
like the rough wool we spin at home.
I wear buckskin now myself and moccasins
traded with the Cree. The women work them
with porcupine quills, delicately dyed,
and with coloured wool and beads when they
can get them. I consider the women beautiful
in their own way, quick and clever. They walk
for miles without complaint, and can ease
a birchbark canoe upriver with the flick
of a brown wrist. Some Company men
take Indian wives to help them stay
alive. The women have shown me the way
they prepare and shape the skins, but all
their skills will vanish, they will vanish.
I'll set down as much as I can. You'd marvel
at how rich they are with so little. Soon
I'll return to the Bay, and before the ice
closes the ocean I'll sail home
to look for a lass in Glen Lyon to be my wife.

David Kinloch

I Presume

In this Opera my Dad is Doctor
Livingstone lost in inclement bush
and I am Stanley trying to think
what I will say to him across the rapids
of our handshake.

It is Act 3: a bank of krieglights
blanch unstinted draughts of a water-hole
putrid with the stage-designer's
vision of rhinoceros dung.

I am in the pit of doubt
unwinding a recitative:
"Commit thy way unto the lord
and he shall direct thy steps."
I stumble on the phrase:

"Is this all gammon?"
And on cue my head turns
back: "Dr Living
Stone, I presume":
a statement of his presence.

He seems to die before me:
unaccompanied, he crumples
on the sedgy grass but then
the hell of music takes him
for the Don he is:

Bramble papyrus thick as a wrist
wraps about his feet as he
Arpeggios down like hippos
of the flooded valleys,
entering embezzled 'discoveries',

The humid theatre of his past
where he arranged "beyond
every other man's line of things"
Ritornellos of rivers,

navigable highways to arias
of liveable plateaux: fantasies
of a fake missionary
and missionary murderer!

I presume your family craved an ending
to the hundred and seventy-six

verse psalms of greasepaint
rife with prodigious ticks and lice,
recognition that the tales of

falls were true. I presume
your son devoutly wished
God's song would stop:
it finally did

And in the darkness
emanating from the flies
we discover a silence
at the heart of music,
even in the silent stave.

I sleep upon one note of hope:
that brief strain –
was it prologue or flashbacked
epilogue? – those tears
when you dropped your oatcake
in the burn at Hamilton.

Pagliacci

Tonight, Svetlov thrusts
his bearded bass into Babi Yar:
"It seems that I am a boy in Byelostok,
that I am Dreyfus"
and yet blood barely stains
sweetie munchers of the Concert Hall,
young couples, sweatered from the same ball of wool,
coughers coughing for the sake of it
and not from the ice cold
breath as it escapes
the chambers of his voice
escapes them as it must.

That night, Dad Pagliaccied
our front room with his stentorian baritone,
frightened his small sons
back beneath a tent of sheets
behind the pink settee,
coaxed them out to hear their father
with a paunch of stockings
our mother knitted up for him.

And there on the savannah
before the piano stool,
we clapped the monstrous

hunchback of our Daddy,
knowing it was Daddy

then blinked and ducked
within the tiny ghetto
of our encampment,
– opera within a minor opera –
plugged our ears
against the way his tears
went major,
flicked shut the flap
against the furnace of his voice
and took each other's hand
in our cool space.

Tonight, Svetlov takes
the flounce of Brussels lace
upon his face, the jab
of parasol, of boot and nail.

He sounds the soundless
scream that we must hear
within the comfort of our concert
tent whose mammoth walls
quaver with Mum's shadow
passing gently like the Magi
over the steppe of Babi Yar
and the weeping wildebeest
of my little brother
"I am Anne Frank!"
"Nò! Pagliaccio non son!"

A Great Adventure

Baby clothes hang on twine
between forked twigs
stuck in Mabota mud:
David Livingstone is not married yet
and has no children to dress.
But he is sure this 'present'
will set his mind to it.

'Sin' in Sichuana is 'cow dung'
and 'holiness', a 'nice fat ox or cow'.
Will he wither in Bechuanaland
or advertise for a 'decent sort of widow'
in the Evangelist Magazine?

Dad faces a similar dilemma
one century later: over Bridge

in the Student Union feels
instinct with promise
but senses his great years
may never come and the switch

from Medicine to Law
not measure up to
Biggles, Hornblower,
Ralph in a Coral Island.

Dad forgets the boredom of great
adventures. How much of it
is simply waiting for the Rains to stop
amid little idol huts, wait-a-bit
Thorns and Logarithm Tables,

forgets how Livingstone's great
'Discoveries' are rarely those he thinks:
His dream – the Nile's source
in the Fountains of Herodotus –
located in an inexistant space
of seventy square miles
conjured by a chronometer he's dropped.

Dad curses the daily circle
of the blue train into work,
rates himself a Failure,
while Livingstone cannot foresee
the extent of an Empire he's suggested
but feels it in predestined bones
and appraises his success.

It is the other way around:
Dad delves the frenzy
of a youthful cancer that warns him early
his life could well be short
and seeks in Grand Italian
Opera the images of heroes
he knows himself to be.

While Livingstone preaches uselessly
to scatterings of Africans,
Dad thrills the Gorbals punters
with minor Donizetti.

While the Makololo dub
'Bokolella', the psalms David
'Bellows like a bull',
Dad bedecks the lives
of fans with the baubles of good tunes.

When we go together
on that voyage into Town
it's the Arch-Druid, Orovesa,
who gets our tickets checked,
the High Priest from Lucia
who processes Union Street.

Macbeth and Malatesta,
Bide-the-Bent from Lammermoor,
all father me upon the ever-
changing stage-set of our house,
so when I become Queen
Anne Boleyn he doesn't lose the head.

Back in Balonda country
Abraham's about to slaughter Isaac
in Livingstone's magic lantern show.
A terrified audience tries to dodge
the knife of faith
he'd insert in their skulls.

He is expelled,
this 'man of sea-cloth',
with his 'little stilts of fire',
his 'hairclaw' and a god
who only descends to die.

An Unpublished Fragment of *Lucky Poet*
Hugh MacDiarmid

Human nature is everywhere the same, but the wilder it is, the more virtuous – Ralph Waldo Emerson

It was when, in 1908, as a boy of 14 I left Langholm and went to Broughton Junior Student Centre in Edinburgh that I immediately began that passionate love affair with Scotland that has continued unabated ever since, a love affair of a kind and intensity akin to Vladimir Soloviev's for Lake Saima in Finland, with this difference that, proverbially, "bitin' and scartin' are Scots folks' wooin'", and my own *affaire* has been justly enough described in *The New Atlantis* by a writer who says:

> He has the defects of his qualities: if he has high enthusiams and stern intellectual discipline his condemnations are often unnecessarily cruel, and his invective inspired less by critical justice than by a foaming wrath that arouses sympathy for the victims rather than for the canons of taste they may have violated. For Grieve hates Scotland as he loves here, hates her weakness and cowardice, her mean love of material comfort and security, and he dare not spare her if she is to awake out of the lethargy of her death-sleep in the snow of her own cold 'native caution'. If Grieve continues to curse and embrace his country in the proud and prodigal fashion that he has made peculiarly his own, who knows but that the Princess of Scotland, she of whom Rachel Annand Taylor wrote: "O who are you that so strangely work/ And raised a fine hand?" may wake to life again in youth and loveliness. We who believe in her and love her fight on in that faith.

There are probably not two Borderers more utterly different in every respect than Margot Asquith (Lady Oxford) and myself; but in her *Autobiography* she repeatedly stresses the keener intellectuality of the Scot as compared with "the Southern English", and she also in one passage quotes the saying that there are two kinds of men – those who give life, and those who only take it. I had no doubt at 14 either of the superlative keenness of my intellectuality or of the fact that I was an altogether unusually vital and vitalising person, destined to "light fires in many cold rooms". I had, in fact, "the talisman of self-sufficiency". Excited as I was in getting to a wider world, I did not like Edinburgh then any more than I do now – when I regard it as little more than "a place to get drunk in". I sensed from the very start its inadequacy, its failure, its bogus role as the Capital of my country, and it neither then nor since ever gave me the feeling of being at the centre of anything. Scotland would be an infinitely healthier and happier place – and incidentally far more Scottish again – at once, if Edinburgh could by some miracle simply disappear off the earth some night, lock, stock and barrel, as if it had never been.

However, all that was not so clearly defined in my mind as it is now. Edinburgh was part of another Scotland, and I frequently cycled the 70 miles between it and Langholm. I had begun to know Scotland, to appreciate a few of our intranational differences, and thus to initiate that process of getting to know all those local variations and "see Scotland as whole" which has since been my main concern – that ultimate complete revelation of Scotland ... which is like Gerard Manley Hopkins' passage in his Note-Book concerning the flag-flower from bud to bloom: "Each term you can distinguish is beautiful in itself and of course if the whole 'behaviour' were gathered up and stalled it would have a beauty of all the higher degree" ... I stress this need alike for an all-in view and for a thorough appreciation of local differences because it is the key to so much of my own work ...

I have already mentioned the effect of the frontier spirit, and the acute perception of differences between places near each other on the Borders, and certainly by the time I went to Edinburgh I attached great importance to demarcations of dialect, and to local shibboleths and the like, and might well have exclaimed, as Djuna Barnes does in her novel *Nightwood*:

> If you think that certain things do not show from what district they come, yea, even to an *arrondissement*, then you are not out gunning for particular game, but simply any catch, and I'll have nothing to do with you! I do not discuss weighy matters with water wits! ... Your *gourmet* knows for instance from what water his fish was snatched, and he knows from what district and to what year he blesses his wine, he knows one truffle from another, and whatever it be Brittany root or if it came down from the North, but you gentlemen sit there and tell me that the district makes no difference.

Not only did my knowledge of different Scottish dialects begin to develop, but my knowledge of foreign languages. I have said that multi-lingual interests were almost hereditary; certainly they developed greatly after I went to Edinburgh, and have ever since been one of my main concerns and are an important characteristic of all my work. It might be said of me as was said of the late Harold Williams that I can claim to have been actuated continuously by the very same spirit:

> Languages, grammars, all the ramifications of philology opened to him as if a magic hand had revealed the realm of words, English and foreign, and led along the paths of philology, steep and stony for most of us, full of colour and harmony for him. He always remembered this sudden sense of inner revelation, of blissful release, as one of the happiest moments of his life ... Mezzofanti himself would have scratched in a match with Harold Williams. This gift of tongues was not an end in itself. Sir Samuel Hoare rightly recognised that it was "the evidence" of wonderful sympathy with human nature in all its forms – a sympathy that "unlocked for him the secrets not only of the tongues but of the hearts of many peoples."

The languages I had to learn were Latin, French, and Anglo-Saxon; but already I was laying the foundation of an ability to read Italian and Spanish too, and, as at Langholm so now in Edinburgh, I was reading terrifically. My school essays of that time show me to have been tremendously under the spell of the modern French poets – Mallarmé, Rimbaud, Verlaine, René Vivien, Comtesse de Noailles. But I recollect that I and a chum of mine, who was killed at the first battle of Loos, used to go cycling all over the country, but especially in Berwickshire, at the weekends, and camping out in a little Spanish silk bivouac tent I had acquired, and that it was at this time that I first got to know the work of many of the younger German, French, and Belgian poets – Mörike, Richard Dehmal, Rainer Maria Rilke, Georg Trakl, Hofmannsthal, Gerhardt Hauptmann, Else Lasker Schuler, Peter Baum, and many others, finding their work infinitely more exciting than anything that was being done at that time in Britain. We were both great admirers, too, of Charles Doughty. I must have had access to his *Dawn on Britain* (1906), *Adam Cast Forth* (1908) and *The Cliffs* (1909) immediately they appeared. ... Other writers first encountered about that time who have influenced me greatly were Nietzsche and Dostoevsky.

My first surprise in Edinburgh was that I was entirely adequate to it. I had no sense of having "heather in my hair" – no self-consciousness at all – such as generally afflicts a country-bred child on first coming to a city. No doubt this was due to the great amount of reading I had done in Langholm – I was not likely to meet (and in fact did not meet) any city child a hundredth part as well read. I immediately became a leader at the school – especially in the Literary and Debating Society, editor of the school magazine, and principal prizewinner in all the subjects that interested me, especially English Literature and History, and Science. I was hopelessly bad at mathematics, and it was not until several years later that I rigorously applied myself to this and overcame my initial handicap in this connection, publishing certain papers involving an utilisation of higher mathematics ...

Immediately on arriving in Edinburgh I had rejoined the Independent Labour Party and, a little later, the Edinburgh University Fabian Society, and began to get a thorough grasp of the literature of the working class movement to which, prior to that, I had belonged in the most passionate way without any such systematic indoctrination. The leaders of the Edinburgh University Fabian Society at that time were extremely able young fellows, almost all of whom were killed in the War; I do not think a group of anything like similar calibre has come together in Scotland since. One of the few survivors was Mr William Graham, MP, and, for a time, Chancellor of the Exchequer. Graham and I (though temperamentally we had very little in common) were good friends and remained so, and frequent correspondents, until his death, though long ere that I had ceased to have any use for, and, indeed, had begun to appreciate the terrible dangers of, mere Reformism and was beginning to go over to the Marxist position. Though the Fabian Society and the Independent Labour Party I had access to a great many books, pamphlets and periodicals of the Socialist and Labour Movement and read these avidly. ... It was at this time, too, that I graduated as an open-air speaker – under the wing of old 'Jimmy' Buchanan, an Edinburgh scavenger and well-known Socialist worker, and of a notorious atheist speaker called McAra, whose addresses were as full of swear-swords [sic] and obscenities and an utter savagery of spirit as if they had been some of the expurgated passages of from Céline's *Mort à Crédit*.

The late Professor James Seth and Professor Charles Sarolea were also, I remember, among the leading members or associates of Edinburgh University Fabian Society at that time. Indeed, on joining it, I recall that I was scrupulous enough to ask Professor Sarolea if I were really eligible.

Another Scotsman I would like to have known is William Livingston, (Uilleam MacDhuinleibhe), an important Gaelic poet, and an isolated fore-runner of the militant Scottish separatists and Anglophobes of today, to whose fine work and original importance I have referred to in my essay on Donald Sinclair (Dómhnall Mac-na Cearslaich) – who happily I did know – in my volume of essays *At the Sign of the Thistle* (1934). Incidentally Common, Murdoch, Mackan and Livingston are – significantly enough – all excluded from the *Dictionary of National Biography*, or, at all events, from the *Concise* edition of it which I happen to have by me.

These, then, are some of the great Scotsmen I would most like to have met, but almost unaccountably failed to, just as, later, I was to meet almost all the living Irish writers but failed to meet one I should have preferred, if I had had my choice, to met rather than most of those I did. I refer to Padraic O'Conaire, the Gaelic storyteller, who died in the fall of 1928, of whom my friend F R Higgins has written, in a most beautiful poem:

> Dear Padraic of the wide and sea-cold eyes –
> So lovable, so courageous and noble –

But, though I lament these signal exceptions, I of all men can hardly com-plain, for I know of few other men, or women either, who have been alive during my lifetime, at least in England, Scotland and Ireland, of whom I knew and whom I would particularly like to have met, whom I have not in fact met and, in scores upon scores of cases, known long and intimately. And yet … three of the exceptions, Maclean, Davidson, and O'Conaire, are so overwhelming, that all my good luck in hundreds of personal meetings with others whose personalities and work I greatly esteem does not rec-oncile me to my bad fortune in respect of these most coveted three.

Edinburgh gave me two experiences of a sort I had not come by in Lang-holm at all – drama and dancing. I saw Sir John Martin Harvey in *Oedipus Rex* and Maeterlinck's *Blue Bird* and a week's repertoire of Ibsen's plays. But more intense and indelible than the impression these made upon me was the effect of seeing Anna Pavlova dance. I made a fool of myself, for I had gone with a girl student with whom I was passionately in love (I have not seen or heard of her for over 20 years, but my blood still lights up whenever I think of her, and I think frequently, and with unabated delight in her beauty as I visualise her again) and … I fainted clean off with sheer excitement as I watched Pavlova dance. When I came to I had to go home to my lodgings. But I went back to the theatre the following night and by taking a tight grip on myself was able to watch Pavlova through her whole performance, though I was excited to a literally dangerous degree, and it took me all my strength and cunning to avoid a repetition of what had hap-pened the night before. I was a nervous wreck for days after – and all the more so because I had spent all my pocket money and had to go for at least a week without cigarettes, which I had this time taken to smoking at the rate of up to 80 a day. A little later, however, I took to the pipe, which was better for me, and much cheaper.

National Library of Scotland

supporting Scotland's written heritage through

The Callum Macdonald Memorial Award

(for poetry pamphlets)
sponsored by the Michael Marks Charitable Trust
and assisted by the Saltire Society

The Robert Louis Stevenson Memorial Award

(for published writers of fiction, poetry,
travel and children's books)
jointly supported by Scottish Arts Council and NLS

The NLS/ Saltire Society Research Book of the Year Award

(for original scholarly research in Scottish subjects)

In addition to these annual awards, the National Library
of Scotland acquires manuscripts and archives of
Scottish writing by gift and by purchase

For further information contact the Library on
0131 622 4807
or email events@nls.uk

Diana Hendry

*A Guide takes Henri Rousseau on a Tour of the
Glasshouses of Edinburgh's Royal Botanic Garden*

Colours? You want bright colours?
Let me show you the Glory Bush. Its flowers
remind me of purple satin. Perhaps you'd prefer
the Scarlet Bugler from Java or the coral pink
of the passion flower? Here's everyone's favourite –
the bottle-brush plant, such a jolly ochre. And just look
at the Jade Vine! Peppermint green I'd call that.
See how it dangles its claw-like flowers?

Tigers have claws too? Indeed, sir. Let's move on
to the Palm House. You think you've seen one?
Eating an antelope? Well it *is* dark and steamy.
We have curly palms, kentia palms, cabbage palms
and this one trying to escape through the ceiling,
is *Sabal bermudana,* the Indian fan, at least
two hundred years old. Now the antelope's crying?
Well it's not surprising. Oh! Spot the bananas!
Monkeys? Eating oranges? No. Not in our plan.

You like the exotic? Well, let's say hello
to the Amazonian lily, the sacred lotus,
and these huge, wild ancestors of the African violet.
You can see a dark woman playing a flute?
And snakes sliding out of the trees? One's draped
round her neck? Best to stay calm, sir.
The lady's often here at dusk – *femina et serpens* –
quite a common species. Shall we run?

Upmarket

Clan chief wants 15 million for Cuillin – The Sunday Times

Now that we have sold the mountains
we are putting on offer Patches of Sky.
We have an excellent variety: Greek
Blue, African Sunset, the ever popular
Streaky Bacon and Mainly Mackerel.
Starry Night is top of the range. Clouds,
being necessary to keep your patch clean,
are supplied in packs of four. A few
small Patches are available for rent or
you might like to consider a Patch Share.
Easy term mortgages can be arranged
with Apollo dot com Parnassus.

Flocks of swallows/sparrows/gulls
are an optional extra. Forget gardens.
Plant your Sky Patch with kites,
balloons, cherubs or our special
inflatable choir of angels.

Customers are reminded that it may
be necessary to police your Patch.
Squads of Patch Watch helicopters
can be hired on an annual basis.

Cheer Leader

You wouldn't want him in your house.
Not that blithe spirit. Not those jollies –
Morning Blossom! Stay positive!
Voice never lower than a shout.
Consider the way he treats the pool
like his own front room, chatting up
old ladies, flexing his pecs at the blonde
attendant. Note that glint in his goggles.
And then there's the performance
with the towel and the songs – *Sometimes
I wonder why I spend the lonely night* –
and *I'm getting married in the morning.*
We wish he was. And yet, and yet

at 8 am on a winter Monday
when the very idea of swimming twenty lengths
is enough to make you call Depressives Anonymous,
he's your heart-throb. *Morning Blossom! Stay Positive!*

Anticipation

I'll leave them folded in my shoes,
resting delicately on my blue socks.
I'll wait until the very last moment.

The outline of everything's softened.
Nothing has a cutting edge.
Even my toes look kinder.

Soon! When I'm dry, when
I'm dressed, I'll lift them
from their nest of socks

and know the miracle
I used to imagine might happen
before I died. Maybe

on top of a mountain
or looking out to sea
or waking one morning

to a moment like this one
when I put on my specs
and all is revealed.

Sandhills Time

They lay between our old home and the sea –
Swoops and falls of pure Saharan sand
Where we played nomads, (camels left elsewhere)
Or desert fathers wise in mystic ways.

Sometimes you'd see it – wind's slow work,
The lift and drift of veil on veil of sand.
So old these dunes they'd sunk a forest, now
It was the air-raid shelter's turn. Ten years

It took to fill its carcass up, wedge shut
Its door for good. We nomads trekked off home.
We'd studied sandhills time. Infinity
Spun round our heads, our steps were lost in sand.

The Romantic Couple: a Fantasy

They ask me the way to the river.
She's from Latin America. There's a century
of flamenco and fiesta in her face. On the corner
of a Scottish street castanets start clacking
in a swirl of petticoats. He's a professor.
His shoulders are bent with the weight
of philosophy. In the cool of a medieval
courtyard he murmurs Cervantes.

They ask me the way to the river
and such a longing comes over me
as if Segovia had picked up my heart
and used it to strum *Humorada*.
Take me in! I want to say. *Take me
into your lives. I'm kith, I'm kin!*
I show them the way to the river,
set off in the opposite direction.

O my dear lost loves,
ask me again the way to the river,
the way to anywhere,
the way to the past.

Andrew Philip

An Independent Light
for Alex Burrough

I catch the light decreasing over Old Town,
honeying buildings black with centuries of reek,
with car exhaust and sovereignty debates.

It calls to mind our evenings, winter into spring,
mingling the light of art and laughter
with malt and hops; a *deoch an doruis*

of Belgian fruit beer I left unfinished,
heavy on the stomach, settled, like the will
of the nation where we double-yessed our friendship.

*

Like a swatch of the second coming,
the sky flickered; lightning released from its
truculent union with thunder and rain:

an independent light. Circling back
towards Wageningen, we became
a colony of dusk. Dissolving into pure

conversation, we were complicit
in music from the nearby shadow of a copse,
conspirators in the clarity of sound.

*

Late-evening lights on the *gracht* in Leiden
– candles, sodium, neons – cast their ballots
for the dark canal where we had found a table.

The strongest light around – your eyes –
devolved its wavelength to your voice
which even then was gathering momentum

for tomorrow's polling day, when you
would *yes* your casting vote in the creation
of a lucid and celebrated union.

Wageningen; Leiden: towns in the Netherlands. *gracht* (Dutch) a street built on either side of a canal.

Meditation on a Cut-price Set of Crockery

Barely half a year of use and yet
the glaze is cracking in these plates and bowls.
They seem as smooth as the day we bought them,
but underneath, we trace the daily strains:

moments when the many waters get so hot
a hairline fracture opens in your tone of voice;
moments when you clatter from my grasp
and hit the bare, hard floor beneath.

Love, it's damaged crockery like ours
that graces the top table in glory –
fit to hold the freshest bread,
fit to hold the best new wine.

A Fundamental Difference

Striding up to us after church like Agabus
an American lady asks my parents

Is that your son? I watched him in the service.
God said to me: That boy is possessed.

Exhorting faith for my brother's deliverance,
the American lady says to pray and does.

(Later, she will tell us how God said to her
I say unto thee – Lindisfarne!,

tell us she knew of no Lindisfarne,
then her husband combed it from the map.)

My parents fold their years of pain into prayerful hands.
Her husband honks in with *Yes Lord!*s and *Amen!*s.

I stand like a spot the lightning is about to strike.
My brother paces, rocks and hums to himself

Jesus loves me, this I know
for the Bible tells me so.

(Later, I will tell you how he sings and hums
anything from hymns to *Starsky and Hutch,*

tell you with what simplicity he speaks to God,
and how he gulps communion down like a dying wish.)

The Road from Emmaus

Were not our hearts burning within us
while he talked with us on the road?

And, suddenly as he came,
he disappears,

                leaving us

like timbers

                glowing after conflagration,
apt at any moment

                  to collapse;

or red-hot iron

                hammered into shape,
aware

        that, as we cool,

                  we harden.

A Voice is Heard in Ramah

I have to trust him now:
his dreams and sense of direction:

we heard the death squads and screams
as we stole out the town,

could hear smashed doors
and fruitless attempts to resist,

could hear inconsolable mothers sobbing,
and the exhausted silences of their men.

We could hear it all for ages
as we picked our way over rocks and scrub.

Hardly a word has passed between us since.
What could we say with all that behind us,

and knowing that our boy – my boy –
the boy who I huddle, feed and coorie doun –

is the one they were after,
the cause of all that death?

Roddy Lumsden

Little Fife – a Road Poem

after Kathleen Ossip

Mind and get in behind that gritter. The Romans did *sut*
make it this far North! Stewing juniper pickles the wind.
I'm fair puggled after going the messages. I'm told Robinson
Crusoe was born in a but'n'ben down that lane. *Jings!*

The guide-book says the chippy has changed hands
in Newburgh. No white pudden. The town no longer
even smells of lino. A golden eagle's been spotted moping
out by Hazelton Walls and a puma sniffing the mean streets

of Methil. Mary Queen of Scots lifted her skirts here. *Shoosh!*
It was just the golf-ball sized hailstones on the windscreen
woke you. Wee fuds skoosh into the wood's edge. *Sorry,*
the onion bridies are done, will half a mince round

do you? It's half day in Windygates so away and comb
monkeys. Your first cairn is an occasion, I grant you, but
by the fifth, you're *like that. How huge is that bing?*
Hang on, we're getting near Kilconquhar where the Cooncil

are building Little Fife, the whole Kingdom in miniature. Is that
a haar or is it just me? *Get that! A hitcher wi' a sign*
saying DUNDEE. The Singing Kettle going techno is jist
deep down tragic. *As I've said before, Vettriano is much more*

than a MacHopper. You've got to give a limpet a right good kick.
Scotrail welcomes you to Leuchars station. *I used to love*
the waltzer like, but these days I'm that gruey. Sunny spells
are promised later. *I hate hats but I'll hae tae hae a hat.*

Evidence of Owls

Unthinkable spoors,
bad jewels laced with a trinkum of mouse-spines
and the black jeel eyes of creeping things.

One wing feather,
a blade of cream, tan, honey, amber, ochre,
flutters on the turf wall of a bunker.

A starter's car arrives,
its headlights flooding two infernal eyes
wheedling the clubhouse and the whins.

This conclusive crescent
where a lilt of static still seethes and cozens:
a gap in the dawn air over Kittock's Den.

A Saltire

Two churnfuls of first milk flushed
across a farmland, night-time sky –
the cross flag juts and fluthers
over a St Andrews bay,
unworked by jibs and rudders,
but undone by small, hard waves, its sheen
mingles, one moment skirting-board grey,
the next the tones of a chic silk stole.

Here, where a saint's bones still knock
in the broth, in current-chiselled troughs
ten fathoms down, where last squibs
of fluorine sea-light
dance off dark hulks of rock,
igniting the shells of sculling shrimps,
kicking their frills from relic to relic,
rolling in a thousand acre feet of swell;

humerus, canine, patella brought to us
at *the north-west ends of the earth*
by Regulus, mad dreaming monk
or money maker,
shipwrecked sailor shivering in his cave,
shaking the salt spray from his hair
and weeping for a handful of bleached,
Greek fingers the bay still crosses for luck.

Perfumes of Scotland

–**Katabella** running shoeless up the snow-chilled burn – **Trinquet** behind the ears of the minister's wife as she trowels the pebbly earth beneath the buddleia – **Scrufan** at midday, breathe in the scent of brickfields stumped along the disused branch line – **Gussie** a scarlet kiss by the dry dock – **Whishie** the wildcat marking the waylanes of his province – **Bomacie** the night filling and fusing as we lie dizzy on the dyke with a bottle, a sputter of static – **Dunino** pine-sap, coot-call, roe-trail – **Truelins** the night tide rooting through banks of shells – **Ferintosh** treacle baccy smoke betraying the beater drawn in to the shady abature – **Wildrif** danced out, half-dressed and gasping – **Immer** for widows only, worn as far afield as Meg's Craig, Latheronwheel and Damnaglaur – **Smitch** a petrol spill in a car park at the back of the rink – **Floshan** fresh dew on the fifteenth green, the flag charmed by the first of the breeze – **Aiverin** moss on a picture book thrown in the stank – **Okraquoy** sweetroot breaching the breakwater, muscling through cracks in the pier – **Merrigle** a tenement tap left on an hour till the water is gospel cold –

Winston Churchill

Mark Barbieri

Whether or not Germany would have won the Second World War if the
6th Army had held Stalingrad is of no concern whatsoever to Simpson. All
he's concerned about is the wind-up and when Tommy's around he's in
his element. Tommy, a committed war historian and a good wee soul in
most respects, does have one major character flaw: he's a helluva Nazi
bastard. As such, Simpson feels that the wee man deserves to get the piss
taken out of him whenever possible. Simpson doesn't know his Leben-
sraum from his Lederhosen but he does know the golden rule: it doesn't
really matter if you're right or wrong, just as long as you sound as if you
know what you're talking about you'll fool most people. And there's
always plenty of fools willing to listen to you in The Anvil.

Now wee Tommy is extremely knowledgeable about the 6th Army's
defensive capabilities but completely useless when it comes to defending
the indefensible. Nobody wants to hear about what might have been,
especially when the would-be victors murdered six million Jews. Simpson, under a heavy verbal assault, claims the moral high ground and
plants his standard firmly into the heart of Tommy's argument.

– In conclusion, Nazi Germany could never huv won the Battle of Stalingrad for the simple reason that Stalin had mair men than Hitler tae waste
as cannon fodder. Now correct me if ah'm wrang, but an infinite supply
ae Cossacks is always gonnae triumph over a few Krauts battling not just
with a flawed ideology, but with a Russian winter cold enough tae freeze
the baws off a bald eagle.

– A bald eagle? But that's Ameri …

– And as I said, there's the concentration camps tae contend with.

– Eh? There's nae talkin' tae you.

Tommy sighs then downs the remainder of his pint. The assembled
drinkers melt away when they realise he isn't going to mount a counter-
attack.

– But d'ye really think Germany hud a chance at all, now that you're
no' playing to the gallery?

– Come off it Tommy, you need your heid examined. You're no a bad
wee bloke but all this Nazi business is a bit much. Ah've got more important things tae worry aboot than Germany winning the Second World War.
Like where ma next beer's coming from for example …

– So, you'll be wanting another pint, then?

– Aye, make it one of those German beers; a Becks'll dae.

A pint of Becks duly appears and Simpson scoops it up enthusiastically.
He takes several large gulps and bangs the glass heavily on the bar.

– Thirsty work this historical debating.

But Tommy isn't listening anymore. The eighth pint has finally kicked
in and he's busy using all his cognitive powers trying to recall exactly what

he's been talking about for the past hour. Another mouthful of beer reminds him that it doesn't really matter and he concentrates on the matter in hand: the barmaid's succulent arse. It's amazing the hypnotic effect a lovely rounded female behind can have to a man under the influence. Wee Tommy's head bobs in unison with its movements like a drooling dog following a dangling biscuit. Poetry in motion, he thinks to himself while dimly trying to recall which poem it most closely resembles. He settles on 'Fat Bottomed Girls' by Queen which isn't a poem at all or even an accurate description of such a sculpted hotpants filler but who cares? It reminds him that all great human endeavours are ultimately doomed to failure and that's poetry enough, especially as she's got a six-foot boyfriend and he's a balding middle aged Fascist, although this is an image of himself he's keen to dispel. Not that it'll help him get into her knickers …

– Ah'm no' a Nazi anyway you. Ah just appreciate the efficiency of the German war machine. It's the same way ah admire the prowess of great empire builders like the Greeks or the Romans.

– You trying to tell me that the fact you own a German Shepherd is a complete coincidence?

– Thousands of people own *Alsatians*.

– Aye, but how many are called Adolf?

– Ah've told you before, the dug was already called Adolf when ah picked him out at the home. Now it's the only name he'll answer tae.

– And how did you know he was called Adolf?

– Ah just kept trying names until ah stumbled on one he seemed tae like.

– Right enough, ah can see how you'd just stumble upon Adolf …

Tommy decides he's had enough of his friend's sarcasm and reverts his gaze to the barmaid's bum, which is the only object in the miserable pub worth a glance. Not to be unfair to the other patrons because the rest of the barmaid is as dodgy-looking as they are, but God has obviously chosen to bless this girl with a posterior worth paying good money for. It's a particularly convenient area to bless given that Tommy's poor, unexamined heid has slumped onto the bar and that her bum now meets his eyeline effortlessly. In a happy daze, Tommy notices that the bottom shelf of the drinks cabinet could probably do with being stocked up …

… a shadow slowly creeps across the bar and Simpson turns round to see Winston Churchill lumbering over the threshold pushing a shopping trolley. Simpson knows that he's normally a level-headed guy and the drink must surely be playing tricks with his faculties. However, everything's there: the short rotund figure; the shabby black overcoat; the chubby cheeks and the cigar welded to the lips. Churchill announces his arrival with the trademark two-fingered salute but Simpson does notice that it seems to be carried off with more venom than the genuine article would surely have intended. He turns to Tommy for confirmation of this aberration and the penny drops.

– Tommy, your wife's here.

Illustration by Shona Dougall

It takes a nudge or two to bring Tommy back from his bouncing reverie and a vigorous shake before his tongue and brain agree to work together.

– Whit the feuck yeugh tawkin' aboot?

– Tommy, it's your Margery, for Christ sake.

Before Tommy has a chance to compose himself and formulate an es–cape plan, he finds himself pinned against the bar by the shopping trolley.

– Ah told ye tae be home at seven. Whit time dae ye call this?

In his intoxicated condition, Tommy still isn't convinced that it is the wife standing before him given her resemblance to our late, great Prime Minister but at close proximity her moustache is a dead give-away.

– Hullo love. Ah wis just thinkin' about ye there.

Her gaze doesn't flicker from Tommy's bleary eyes but the tendons on her neck start twitching and her nostrils begin to flare up like an infuriated bull's. Simpson looks down to check for hooves and notices her leather jackboots. He considers the possibility of a sexual element to Wee Tommy's fascism; however, a quick appraisal of the rest of her provokes Simpson to consider the effect eight pints of beer has on one's judgement. Margery edges menacingly forward and Simpson realises that although Tommy's no matador, his blotchy red face is proving enough of a red rag to this old bull.

– Thinking aboot me were ye? Is that why yer eyeballs were glued tae that wee tert's erse?

– Margery, ah've only got eyes for you, ye know that.

– Don't give me that shite. Ye were supposed tae be home three hours ago no sittin' in this pub gettin' pished. But as God's my witness, yer coming home noo.

Simpson vaguely hopes that if God does exist he isn't wasting his Saturday evening witnessing this pathetic example of human interaction. But his attention is drawn to Margery as she attempts to lay hands on Tommy. Having detained his friend in the pub all afternoon simply to wind him up, he feels compelled to intervene on his behalf.

– Don't be like that Margery. We were engaged in a highly intellectual discussion on Nazi Germany's military capabilities and the consequences for Europe had they won the Second World War.

Margery stops in her tracks and stares curiously at Simpson. He realises his error as a ball of frothy spittle starts to form at one side of her mouth. She starts chewing manically on her cigar before taking a long puff and exhaling the smoke into his eyes. As he recoils in pain, Margery drops her cigar into his pint. The sizzle of extinguishing embers sounds uncannily like the hiss of air escaping from his over-inflated ego.

She turns her attention to Tommy like a butcher sizing up his next carcass. Terror spreads across his befuddled features as Margery sweeps him off his feet and, in one fluid movement, deposits him into the shopping trolley. A tin of baked beans is sent bouncing onto the floor. A beaten man, Tommy seeks diversion in the ingredients label of a Pot Noodle while other drinkers start coughing and examining bits of hitherto undiscovered fluff on their clothes. Margery calmly watches the tin of beans as it makes a bid for freedom Steve McQueen would have been proud of. Simpson decides that appeasement is the better part of valour and grabs the tin and places it carefully in the trolley. She turns to face him.

– Don't give me that German pish. Even the dug is sick of listening to him. It's time he started tae realise that it was the Yanks that pulled the strings in that war. Right from the early days when they guarded the Allied supply lines across the Pacific tae when the Japs invaded Pearl Harbour and brought thum intae the war proper. Then they really kicked Adolf's erse. Aye, America, now that's a nation tae admire …

Simpson looks momentarily confused then regains his composure. He glances at the other drinkers who wonder if he'll dare rise to the bait.

– Aye, right enough Margery. Ah can see your point.

Her eyes flash in triumph as Simpson smiles weakly. Grown men cower in the shadows as she swings the trolley round and blitzkriegs her way out of the pub. The double doors flap Open and Closed and Simpson glimpses his friend clinging to the side of the trolley in terror as Margery embarks on a kamikaze mission across the dual carriageway and heads for the drive-thru McDonalds. He turns to address anyone who'll listen.

– Now let that be a lesson to any budding Fascist: totalitarianism always begins at home.

Lydia Robb

Kate O'Shanter

When chapman billies leave the street
An drouthy neebors, neebors meet;
When market days are wearing late
Just spare a thocht for Tam's wife Kate.

While he was boozin at the nappy,
That spouse o his was nane ower happy;
Myndin bairns, an stuck at hame
While Tam wad flirt wi ilka dame.

She kent him weel, he was a skellum.
Time tae chynge yer weys, she'd tell him.
Tam repented – saa the licht,
"Aa'll tak ye doun the toun the nicht.

Awa'n get ready, dae yer hair,
Ma Maw will babysit am shair."
Nae man can tether time or tide;
The hour approaches Tam maun ride.

Weel mounted on his Kamasaki,
Kate on the pillion, unco happy.
The Mecca hall wis drawin nigh,
Where Bingo callers nightly cry.

Kate bocht her tickets, all the sevens,
Ninety nine and legs eleven.
A Playtex girdle happed her hurdies,
While Tam wis eyein up the burdies.

Kate yelled HOUSE an gart them skirl,
She'd won the jackpot – what a girl.
But only *she* would understand,
The Deil had business on his hand.

She'd pent the toun; she had the siller.
Houghmagandie wi the miller?
In lurex breeks an sequinned sark,
Her duddies skinkled in the dark.

Then oot the blue, oor Tam chynged tack
An on the lasses, turned his back.
His Mither's gizz, soor as a grozet;
She fents when Tam comes oot the closet.

But Women's Lib had taen Kate's fancy,
Up tae 'here' wi Poosie Nancy;
She packed her bags, took aff for Spain
An said that Tam could mynd the weans.

Now, wha this tale o truth shall read
Aa hope you laddies aa tak heed:
Think whit ye value maist in life.
Remember, Tam O'Shanter's wife.

Juanita

Oh yes, they could tell.
  Look at the way she walks,
the anklechain,
  the snakeskin shoes, the skirt
that's slit from thigh to hem.

The old men in the bar
  turn over her past;
tasting her indiscretions
  on their tongues.

Tonight she tempts them
  with her sensual songs.
Do you believe in life after love? ...

The fisherman, who used to be,
  is on his feet.
A snapped hawser left his mind at sea.

His fingernails
  are salted with sardines,
his skin silvered with the trace
  of forgotten fishscales.

He dances lightly in his rubber boots
  to the music of Cher,

Something simmers
  in this foreign place,
implicit as the longing.

Mantra

October morning: air shrivelling to nothing.
This is the perfect day for sucking lemons.

Log on to the iron-will website;
chant the mantra for today.

Better to be thin and dead
than fat and thin.

She makes a note
to rid herself of the wardrobe mirror.

The nearer she gets, the wider
and more unforgiving it becomes.

Only she can see beyond the cheekbones,
skin transparent as tissue and

thighs wish-boned down to size.
Restless as the emaciated cat,

her hands become scales,
weighing the ghost of a future.

Following in his Fuitsteps
efter Seamus Heaney

I read your 'Postscript': made towarts the wast
intae County Clare alang the rocky shore.
It's no September nor October but the wun
an licht are still at odds wi ane anither.
The Atlantic swal on ae side, scatterin
spindrift like thrissledown on Inisheer.
The keekin-gless o lough, a sherp reflection
o wild geese risin in a skinklin prism,
weengs creakin, they whurl towarts Slieve Aughty
their set and soun fadin. Diminuendo.
A puckle cast fedders settled on the watter.

Fancifu tae feel I'll snare yon images
and bring them oot at will. I micht be only
passin this wey aince; aiblins never
again, as the prevailin wuns caa
richt aff coarse and tak me by the thrapple.

Granda Taylor

I can't forget
the image of the child,
her hair the colour
of wet marigolds.

Asthma spoke.
Birds chirping
in the old man's throat.
He wrung the hen's neck;

gave the child
the armour-plated leg,
pulled the tendon
and set the claws dancing.

I cringed under a fat ham strung
from the ceiling. Watch *oot!*
Ye'll gyne bald, he said
if it dreips on your heid.

Rites

The howdie-wife's knowing face,
its intimacy with death.

Imagine: a healthy bairn spirited away
and a trowie changeling in its place,

the lid prised from the sleeping well,
stagnant water salted in its throat.

And then the drowning
before a breath was drawn,

the unplumbed darkness spooling her in
to the ammonite of coiled rib, clenched thumb.

She would deny the labour pains,
the blood stains on bleached linen.

She'd jouk the neighbours and
the kirk elders, inciting confession.

Her conscience played games
endlessly, tears falling

in useless gestures, like rain
from a sky the colour of infinity.

Timing

A lukewarm carry-out
more sour than sweet.

Then, from his box of tricks
he magics a videotape
with the title inked out.

He stops it at the part
where their vows are being made,
switches off the sound,
presses rewind and watches himself

leisurely slipping the ring
from her finger, her father taking
her by the arm and walking
backwards down the aisle,

the bridal taxi reversing
to a slowly fading dot.

Then cut.

Iain Galbraith

couvades

a warm bowl. imagine the burrow in the hollow of his back. this is the
song of the blackbird in ivy creeping up the wall of the house.

a sunday sunlight peeks through the chinks of the blind. no colours he
will remember but later a pool of white light in the corner the music dark
a band like a reptile escaping from a box.

maybe that window. maybe someone playing louis jordan at three in
the bloody morning. five little guys named moe. saturday night no shouting from the other windows the guy who's been complaining not complaining. sad and old in the sleeping town. lullabies. he falls asleep wakes
with her breath tickling his ear.

but they were playing these things now. it was sentimental. in the hollow her big belly the baby at his back pushing in. all three in the quiet
morning with the music chinks of sunlight dotting the cupboard the wall.

big moe little moe someone slams the back door. is this the peace they'll
remember? because he'll want her? now he does. five little guys split
refracted and broke. all you does and all you don't my baby.

and no buts see.

2.

solitude. just lying there maybe asleep maybe listening. or sort of on
stand-by. sea-trout pressing its nose to the current. like he was looking
down into the flightering green under a bridge watching the tight surface
of the pool waiting for the rise the splash the ring.

here he is then looking forward to looking back wondering if he'll want
it back. already knowing he won't. where'll the he go that wants this now.
he'll be here. he'll be another. more. he'll be the crowds. coming out of
nowhere. but that don't mean a thing.

j s bach. steps echo in the close between the walls at the back. on and
on. down the tracks to the nil tunnel of the horizon. in her solitude she
holds him with her memories that never want to die. is that her thinking
of the wee one now? is that him? will they be like this? bach's frantic glassy
sounds. turning him in on himself. short pieces nine little preludes five wee
moes. the white stairs disappearing down a spiral stairwell suddenly green
fire emergency sign green exit sign down down down. racing up the keys
flights intervals landings. is it up is it down is it up the stair going down.
baby. an ellipse whirling to a summit. slowly slowly. stately. art of the flight.
all the way. all away. all awake. in the maze of stairs they'll be waiting

3.

with their jabs and bottles and forms. and dark.

why you this and why you that my baby. a lizard and snakes are all he
sees for miles. they might trip fly tumble down head over heels splash
awhile in ruby pools bounce off stone steps and slo-mo. they go. sailing
around the globe. in the plane your belly drops blunt just as they start to

climb again. pressing down further further further till you were faster yourself and the plane slips out the pocket and there they all were in white on a different stair.

and you never do have time to sort. chinks of light. eyes stuck down after long wet sleep. her arms hooked under his.

solitude. sunday morning. blackbird knows. first song presses into his back. all three round-eyed blinking into the day.

The Angel's Share

Twisting duneward
to a sheerer dark

brushing the lips
of roadside pits

he finally escaped –
winged it on a kiss …

Foreshortened by the speed
we pass the other way

bats parabolic over the links
the cat sewn into its nameless bag

tracks to the breakers
that only just come back.

Translator's Note

The empty road, the submerged
density of frozen elms

the travellers stamping their feet –
small hours turned

like pennies to shadow the eyes.
In the shallows broken ice

flounders and clicks. *Rot*
a vowel I've smuggled out

drips to the white path. Reader –
trust me, trust me not!

Is it my doing
if the slopes already

verge on an edge
where the sledge rides with children

end in deeper snow?
Muck-spreaders

work the furrows, beacons
fade on the distant shore.

Sparrows on all the roofs
whistle the answer as we pass.

The Settlement

We are *neozoa*
packed into lodgings
their builder-users quit with cart and hound
bequeathing as they scattered hence
the dauntless gifts they held in song to last
their *old man's face* their *dyers' rock* the sound
beguiles us still as hidden caves
where echoes whisper kings and broken men.

*

High water
blackened the sand – it must have been the day
my nose burned raw and box-crabs in their thousands
crossed the wall to Shore Street.
I remember how my blistered fists paled
as our men clenched the wooden hafts
the keel's fleet shadow in the sunlit depths
strangely flickered on and off the silt
as if inscribing our ungrounded tenure there
translucent fronds fan-shaped and pink
like mockery spread giant wings
in the equivocal flux.

*

I fled along the shore perplexed
and overheard two in the road that joined their hands
Their secret tongue had touched my ear
a wedding havocked thought could not endure.

Flat Stones

What you are thinking
home from the shore
with your salt-scalded
driftwood and hagstones

I shall never know.
How glad I was
we turned
our backs on interdict

contra want of restraint
in exposing a child
to the dying. Granddad
was a kind of hand

you stuck a healing plaster to
fighting to smile through
this door yet.
His widow and children

with these flat stones
cut the trench for his ash.
That day on Gigha
we took to the rockpools

your newly purchased net
but the Plentiful One
kept a fearful distance
till teatime. Once

we walked to the edge
the stones we skiffed
ending and sinking
in the shining bay.

Poplars

A morning left
to final touches

rippling donors
of wind and space
vigilant peaks

*

The calf swims
at the port
of every eye

Aubergine night
floods the plains

*

Slender sisters
keep watch
in silver gowns

In the forest
death is close

*

Dawn opens
purple lips

Nimble hooves
chase darkness
to the hills.

Stardust Disco

Gavin Bowd

Apart from the tides, which are controlled by the position of the Sun and the Moon, the heavenly bodies, as they are called, have nothing at all to do with everyday events on Earth – Children's Britannica

It had been a clear, cold day. Crows had been flying high. When the dying sun caught them, it was like their wings were in flames. Then Venus appeared and night followed. The Earth had completed its orbit around the sun, and it was that time of year again: the Christmas disco at St Peter's Primary School. The Stardust DJ would be back, playing the hits and more obscure tracks from his vinyl collection.

I did not want to go. In the corridor, Siobhan had jibed:

"You're not goin' wi *anyone!*"

Looking at that lovely face, I'd felt a sob seize my throat. But Mum insisted and, as I stretched around my neck the elastic of my tie, I felt like a calf tagged for the abattoir. The road to the school was now glittering with frost. It was pitch black, and big trees were brooding beside me. I did not hurry along. Instead, I looked up at the sky.

From the troposphere to the thermosphere, there was nothing. As I walked and watched, the lights of stars were rushing across centuries to crowd out the sky. Polaris stood there, bright and permanent, but the Moon and the planets were going through phases, and even constellations would change with time. Santa, I hoped, would bring me that telescope.

I reached the gates of the school. The gym was already trembling behind the curtains. I went in and bought a Caramac and a bottle of Irn Bru. Siobhan took my money, but did not look me in the eyes. She was officious, as befitted the manageress of the tuck shop, the pet of the Headmaster, the one all the boys orbited around. *I love to love* sang Tina, and my heart sank. There they all were, in serried ranks: boys and girls, shuffling from one side to another, their flares slightly flapping. Some had invested in platforms. In passing, I could smell whiffs of stolen perfume.

I stood in the dark corner by a radiator. I drew the corner of a curtain, but I could not see the stars. From the stage, lights were flashing across the gym. I looked at the DJ, concentrated upon his work. He was selecting his next disks, and dealing courteously with petitions from the floor.

Siobhan entered the disco. But she was soon followed by the Headmaster. He said something, and she obediently left. I downed another square of chocolate. The track had changed.

> We had joy, we had fun,
> We had seasons in the sun!

I, too, moved for the exit. On leaving, I turned left up the stairs to the girls' playground. There would be no-one around, and the view would be good.

I was glad to live in a small town. It meant that the street lamps could not out-shine the stars. So I stood and looked and waited for them to come.

The encyclopaedia had told me: "When we look at the stars we are looking back deep into the past". And so they came, at 186,300 miles per second. Super-giants and white dwarves, Betelgeuse and Bellatrix, the Ring in Lyra. My eyes were very young, but I could only make out six of the Pleiades. If Santa brought me the telescope, I could see over a hundred. One day, I thought, when I was big as Dad, I could travel to see the southern stars.

The light was on in the Headmaster's office. He was there, and so was Siobhan. I took a swig of the Irn Bru, and walked onto the lawn to get a closer look. The Headmaster was sitting, legs apart. On his lap he had placed a red bag fringed with cotton wool. I was struck by the man's white hair and beard, As far as anyone could tell, they were real. Siobhan looked nervous as she dipped her hands into the bag.

A decade later, Siobhan told the Court that he had asked: "Tell me what you find in Santa's lucky bag."

She dipped in her hands. Her fingers touched two balls hanging in a hairy, wrinkled sack. "What's that? Is it a mouse?"

"I don't know", she replied.

"And what else do you find?" There was a small, sausage-like thing, veined and ridged, which began to stir and stiffen.

"Is it a snake?" asked the Headmaster.

"No, a worm!"

"It's a *snake*," he admonished. "You had better hold on so it doesn't bite!"

And Siobhan held on, until its venom spurted on her blouse.

"Now you go away and clean yourself."

I saw her run out and along to the girls' toilets. I finished my drink and returned to the disco. In Volume 16 of the *Children's Britannica*, 'Seed to Star', there is no entry for 'Sex'. Instead, I was thinking: "We believe that we stand still, and yet, we are travelling at 66,600 miles per hour."

In the gym, the lines of lovers had been reshuffled. Some casualties were crying or puking, others staring blankly at the strobe-smitten. I joined them for the next song. It was Alvin Stardust. *My coo-ca-ca-choo.* We'd all seen him on TV, clad in black leather. His gloved hand dangled trophies of panties and bras. He made me laugh.

Siobhan reappeared. She looked as magnificent and terrifying as ever. She smiled and went over to Simon. They kissed, then joined the metronomic shuffling of the dancers. Next to me, David was crying his eyes out. I, too, was in tears. I said: "I fucking hate discos!"

David concurred, and together we began to flick the Vs at the dancers, the DJ, the lights and the tunes.

When the Stardust Disco died, the heavens still hung over St Peter's. As I left the gates, I looked up at the Moon. To myself I spoke the litany of its barren ridges: Sea of Tranquillity, Sea of Crises, Lake of Dreams. You would have to be an astronaut to see the other side.

I hurried back home. I would have to be fresh for Venus and the school-bell. Some tears would stain the pillow, and I would pray to the ceiling for the tide to turn.

aonghas macneacail

a voyage to christophia

in memoriam chris boyce, most persuasive purveyor of science fact and fiction, trader in laughter bombs, who embraced every world within his reach as if it were a beloved friend

there was this planet,
it wasn't huge but
it wasn't wee,
it was a place of
loud unsleeping cities
and fields like libraries,
it never lacked
the company of planets,
but was drawn into the orbit of
those two bright stellar
radiances, fun and knowledge,
there was no big show,
it didn't need the usual flags,
the laughter and the facts
burst forth like
roses, salmon, bright auroras,
it was there, it was then, it will not
be swept beyond our ken

*

on this planet the inhabitants are big
as love, burly with laughter, built like
winter-coats-worn-all-the-year-round but
don't be misled by the bulk and the too
early morning, not-quite-hurried-enough, look,
it's the mask for a mind as busy as rush-hour,
weaving its populous filigree out of a crowded
random street into terse and telling paragraphs

on this planet, language is ludic, deep,
syntax of demon chuckle and celestial
grin, wide and warm as a carnival sea –
thought here is food, information sweet,
more nectarine than lemon, otherwise it's
ripe green grapes, as yeasty as the morning's
news, and everything (to make clear sense
of it) viewed sideways, words spread like trees
and aeroplanes, constellations, tell different stories,
galaxies are deep with possibilities, but
moons are daughters, loved and laughed with, o

the fun of having daughters,
mum's the radiant sun whose hot
and nourishing love all orbit round
fruit of this carefully hoed and harrowed
riddling spin of being, could grow into
a bursting weight of conversations
through harvest night, into the never aging dawn

*

cars would be dangerous on this planet,
they'd growl, kick, refuse to stand in
order, demand to eat flesh, put
their foot down, nitpick, seek to go
in opposite directions, bickering into
the most wonderfully Technicolor
sunsets, with a mischievous smile

but grasses should be short here, make
a space to lie
and look into the deep drawn air
for unpredicted stars

*

in its hot impermanent human shape
this heavenly body is, mostly, a sea of speculative tides
in which great landforms, each with its own
distinctive pulse, burst forth,

one offers flights across both time and space,
one teems with flowers, feasts and questions falling,
bright, like meteors, on the great plains of work

there are no shores to the illumimant continent of a mind
which feeds on lightnings, propels windmills
out, to tilt at ostentatious suns and flagrant stars

– in the continent called home, the familiar
is an embracing field, a familiar
forest of silences and conversations,
unreliable echo says this
embracing field, embracing
field, and memory

king of all this insistent republic,
if it allowed kings, would be
the engine curiosity, and time,
that (curious) elastic, which, simultaneously
extends beyond the bounds of geometry and
folds into this strange, indeterminate, silence,
absence, echo, silence – *listen* –
there's a big broad chuckle in that echo!

why not faith (studies in green)

what the eye sees

a skim of verdigris
      the perfect geometry of
      this dome like half a world
beneath its starburst spine of arches
parasol for balsam words this
   refuge from the harder
                  sentences demanded
in the darker world where garrulous frogs
shrug off the algal fur now blanketing their pool
to leap in droves across arterial
              roads, blood
pulsing for the cleaner stream beyond

the eye sees this,
among stone fluted
trees   within
unmossed and mica-starred
a slow procession pray
for eloquence to blind
the lost with truth,
this few who would be multitude
whose sentences are sung
as webs are spun

above,
into its shade
the copper bowl drinksecho
song and starling scuff and swallow
all   the afterthoughts allowed to linger,
i'll   not tell you what i really
lizards in the undergrowth

behind the heavy door
its timbers steeped in time
rat, rat who's always there
may break   a back
of bread   that's far too old
to set on table
rat may eat   you know
rat's rat, that
rat won't pray, that rats
don't need to pray

Eddie in Edinburgh #2 : A stroll on Arthur's Seat with Aonghas MacNeacail

aonghas macneacail takes Eddie Linden up Arthur's Seat!
cartoon by Gerald Mangan

reflections on the moon

a full moon
      and the way
  a piano can dance yet
at the same time   sound
    so sleepy
       across dark water

    *

a full moon
and
     where the old dog ran
  a dog runs still

    *

a full moon
     and a swan so
transparent in that thin light
it's impossible   to say
    whether
      it sleeps
or   thinks
     to attack

    *

a full moon
     four geese
cannot agree how to shape
their wintering   formation

    *

a full moon
    and there's insistence
    like seaborne winds
that the book should be read
  which tells
how truths are measured

    *

a full moon
    and the smatter of
     running feet
under shadow trees

    *

a full moon
and
     in the still bowl of the bay
find   a full moon
imperceptibly   dancing

*

a full moon
and   nothing new
    under the sun
                waving incidentally
        in the soft breeze

*

a full moon
            yes please daddy
says the child who knows
the possibility
                    always exists
for more

*

a full moon
    the thought slides
        out of reach
    along a stream of mirrors

*

a full moon
and on this field
        a narrative
    of human blood
            where grasses should have grown
        an owl alone
plays flute   against the still grey night

*

a full moon
    not even the ghost of a breeze
so   why this grit in the shoe
                this grapeseed lodged between teeth

*

a full moon
    the spider leaves a mesh
    wide as a bridge
a dog would cross in search of bones
becoming its own carrion
            this is a dream poem
            the dog may choose   not to enter

*

a full moon
        snarled by clouds
if there's a time   for saints and wolves then
        this is it

on wolfe tone quay, dublin 1998

that dove
among the grass
as gray and still as
stone
unlikely ghost
of all the geese
returned to die
for this
and those blackbirds
who stayed to
sing concordant songs
in all the riven times of
storm and hate
for this
for this

two hundred years
this melody
lives in the grass

and if the dove's
gray wings
could pluck an anthem
from
the harp uncrowned
those ghosts
would rise and dance
there's work
still to be done
they'd say but we can
dance and sing
that old concordant
song again
for this

the dove is
tentative
among the grass
is listening
for this
is listening
for this

the noise
of making new
is
thunder in the ear

biscuit sun

the bright red
wrapper makes
a sun on that grey
table, biscuit
energy that all
our hungers orbit,
all our teeth prepared
to slowly die
among its active
radiant sugars,
being young this
once, alone, we
know that we can
spin into the
kind embrace of
other, safer, suns

but now, bright disc
of melting joy, we
know your light alone
will feed, will burn

on birth

in the crimson interval between
that blind surging moment
and the first shadow of motion,
a plunge into alien cool air,
and instantly,
so much activity,
so many hands,
the novelty of cloth

The Language of Poetry

Franco Loi

translated by Heather Scott

Speaking of his own poetic experience, Paul Claudel distinguished, or rather, adopted an ancient distinction between two elements in man's inner being: *animus* and *anima,* sometimes calling the former *spirit.* We could also call it *animus*, although imprecisely, because other elements converge there too, the intellect, individual rationality:

> Anima is unlearned and simple, has never been to school; while Animus knows an endless number of things, has read great quantities of books ... One day, when Animus came back unexpectedly, he heard Anima singing all alone, behind a closed door, a strange song, something that he did not know ... Then Animus tried to make her sing again. But Anima falls silent as soon as Spirit looks at her ...

The Spanish mystic, Theresa of Avila, wrote in her *Interior Castle:* "Observe this soul (anima) that God has made entirely without intellect, the better to imprint in her true wisdom ..." And Dante:

> As one who sees while dreaming
> and when the dream is gone the passion stamped
> remains, and nothing else comes to his mind again ...

The similarity between the two states (the mystic and the poet) begins therefore in the "sleep of the intellect" – a state of abandonment of the being by means of which the active force becomes emotion, while the intellect dwindles to a presence, a watchful element, and becomes a superconscious entity or detached observer of the whole movement.

Again Dante says, turning to Apollo:

> Enter my breast and breathe
> as when you drew Marsyas
> from the sheath of his limbs.

Another aspect is the meeting of consciousness with a deep part of ourselves, where what we may provisionally call the *unconscious*, presents itself as *other* (alter), as a force independent of our *ego*, an ulterior presence, often no more than a fleeting stirring of the mind or a shadow or an inexplicable certainty, which nevertheless, as we discover in poetry and psychology, has its own laws and its own proportions, an order of its own that is not that of the intellect nor that of our feelings, nor yet of the *ego*.

Perhaps it was in this sense that Hölderlin wrote: "It is no bad thing for man to measure himself against divinity ..." And Jung observed:

> My psychological experience has demonstrated that certain manifestations come from a psyche more complete than that of which one is conscious... Often they contain in themselves an analysis, an introspective inquiry or a superior consciousness, which the normal consciousness would never be capable of producing at that moment... There is an appropriate word for these cases: intuition... Men never consider the fact that we do not ourselves manufacture intuition. On the contrary, it always comes of itself; one

has a sudden intuition, which is born of itself and only he who is quick can
    grasp it ...
Jung recognises earlier, in these deep levels of the unconscious, the
emergence of archetypes which "have their own autonomous rationality".
    The 17th century Spanish mystic, Antonio de Rojas, said: "God has
placed his image in the most secret part of man, which is the root and the
base of the soul (anima) ..." And Marcel Proust says of a certain character:

> Vinteuil reached with all the power of his creative effort towards that depth
> where, whatever question one might ask of it, it is with the same tone that
> it replies ...

The Jesuit father Souilhe wrote in 1922:

> In the doctrine of Plotinus the means by which the soul reaches the
> supreme object of its desire is that of going back into itself and finding in
> deep concentration the interior God of which it bears the traces ...

This phenomenon relates to every poet, even if in diverse ways, and can,
from time to time, involve the intellect and other faculties, since there are
poets in whom rationality, or reasoning activity, is greater, or predominant;
others in whom emotion or sensation is preponderant; and others in whom
the body and its desires, its passions, predominate. It is certain that in all
of them the poetic activity functions by setting in motion the deepest strata
of the individual, whether he is conscious of it or not. After all this occurs
in every man, as soon as he abandons himself to interior emotion – and
one has only to think of those in the state of being in love.

> Only for me, the solitary one
> shine the infinite stars at night,
> the stone fountain murmurs its magic song,
> only for me, for me the solitary one,
> the coloured shadows of the clouds that pass
> like dreams, move above the countryside ...

wrote Hermann Hesse. And something similar is affirmed by Schopenhauer, too, when discussing the fascination of music.
    What then is the difference between the poet and the mystic, between
the poet and the saint? A scholar has said: "The more men draw near to the
condition of poet in themselves, the further they draw away from the
essence of the mystic in themselves". The mystic, when he enters into contact with the Self, takes possession of it, establishes his individual relationship with it; whereas the poet does not aim at this special form of
possession, sufficient for him is the moment of abandonment and of vision,
the unknown experience and the emotions or stirrings that arise in him.
    So the mystic immerses himself in contemplation, he enters steadily into
the ecstatic condition, there he concentrates with his mind and his will:
silence becomes the primary quality of his experience; the poet on the
other hand does not concentrate his will on the substance, the essence of
the experience, but only on the form, nor does he become totally
absorbed, therefore the essential element of contemplation eludes him.
    While the mystic absorbs in silence – and becomes absorbed by the

voice and by the vision – the poet feels the need to speak, he feels the fascination of the word: the word is the quality of his participation in the experience. Someone once said: "The mystic is silent, the poet speaks."

"One could say" wrote the Protestant theologian Alessandro Vinet, "that the poets have been sent to speak and not to be."

The poet is seized by the wish to recount, to communicate, whereas the mystic is taken up by the experience, and reserves with silence the privilege of becoming possessed by the power that reveals itself to him.

This has been concisely set out by Dante in the *Paradiso*:

I was as one who cometh to himself
from a forgotten vision, and doth strive in vain
to bring it back unto his mind ...

... But whoso thinketh of the weighty theme
and of the mortal shoulder which hath charged itself therewith,
will think no blame if under it it trembleth ...   *(Canto XXIII)*

... and I have seen things
which whoso descendeth from up there
hath nor knowledge nor power to re-tell;

because as it draweth nigh to its desire,
our intellect sinketh so deep,
that memory cannot go back upon the track.   *(Canto I)*

The closer the poet draws to mystic vision, the less he is able to recount it.

The English poet Coventry Patmore: "The poet occupies, in the hierarchy of creatures, a singular position: half way between the saint and Balaam's ass." The word is at the centre of the poet's attention, even if in the poetry the order imposed by the interior movement is more important. "We who have no other happiness/ but words" wrote Camillo Sbarbaro.

But the word, as we have just indicated, is not sufficient for poetry. Dante suggests as much when he says:

All things have order among them,
and this is the form which makes the universe resemble God ...

The relationship of the Poet with the Word cannot ignore the order in which things present themselves, the sequence that springs from emotion.

Cesare Pavese says: "When a man on the sea-shore says 'How beautiful!', this is poetry". But Pavese errs. Poetry does not lie in external emotion, but in interior contemplation, in the speaking moment. Neither the utterance of it, nor reiterating it through feeling, nor positioning it mentally, believing this establishes an intellectual order, is sufficient for qualification as poetry.

The order within which the word presents itself is fundamental, because the word does not reveal itself only in the significant and the signified, but in an order that springs from the movement, or emotion, of the unconscious world that reveals itself: the objective beauty assumed in the subject. By emotion I do not refer to the subjective impression that brings it, but to the *e-motus*, to the objectivity that inspires emotion in the individual.

And so, the silences, the measure of the syllables, the scansions, the assonances and dissonances, that is, all the relationships of rhythm and sound that run through the words are constituents of the reflective order that proceeds from the man and the nature of his relationship with the thing that comes to be said. This order is not imposed by the ego or by the intellect – as the majority of versifiers tend to believe, thinking that by choosing a metre or fixing cadences they are exercising dominion over the matter of the poem – it is not derived from the consciousness of the poet, but is a reflection of the archetypes that, as psychological science has revealed, like to express themselves in symmetrical forms.

Every poet knows that his most natural poetry comes from an intimate relationship between the word and the order that he finds within himself, the order through which the word suggests itself to him or appears to him in the 'making of poetry', in making himself the conduit to poetry.

And all this does not mean that the poet does not make a contribution with his intellect, with his learning and his culture, and even with his particular taste, to the construction of a poem. In fact it is certain that lexical culture, and metrical or musical culture, like general philosophical and literary knowledge, are indispensable to the constant work of refining and correcting, just as taste and general culture are important for the choice and multiplicity of the references. All this work is also necessary in order to furnish the structures of communication applicable to the time, to a given society, to the customary models of learning of a generation.

It is from the accord between the forms suggested by the archetypes and the culture and the knowledge of an individual, within an epoch and a society, that springs the concrete 'self-revelation of poetry'. Three passages, from an essay by Marina Cvetaeva, tell us something of this process:

> The creative condition is obsession. Something, someone, takes possession of you, your hand is only the instrument – not of yourself, but of another.
> Who or what can this be? It is that which wishes to exist through you.

Obsession is perhaps not the right word, because there is contemplation and detachment, and therefore we are not in the area of illness, which today takes up such a large space in the literary field. But the compulsion is stronger then the subjective will; obsession presents itself here as a call, as the unceasing will of an objective presence. Cvetaeva again:

> I hear, not the words, but a sort of silent melody within my head, a sort of sound-track. I am certain, however, that even here, as in everything, there exists a law.

Nadezda Mandelstam writes in her memoirs, *Time and the Wolves*:

> When the work is in progress, nothing can check the interior voice which, I believe, resonates with tremendous power ...
> There is a moment in which the sound is already buzzing in the ears, and the lips, barely moving, seek painfully for the first words ...

And here is the third passage from Cvetaeva:

> For a poet, theory is always *post-factum*, deduction from personal experience, a backward journey along his own tracks. Theory is verification.

The relationship of the poet with the word takes over his entire being, his life, even the order of the world. It is a matter of tension and attention to the essence of his own existence. Through the word one restores order into our relationship with things, with the world. Jaroslav Seifert says:

> Poetry has been with us from the beginning,
> like love,
> like hunger, like the plague, like war …
> I believe that searching for beautiful words
> is better than killing and slaughtering.

Against the order imposed by philosophies, the power of money and violence, poetry sets its own order, aspiring to restore an original relationship, the archetypal order of which religions seek to be the intermediary.

We have sought to testify with the voice of poets to the common interior matrix of poetry and mysticism, the analogies between mystical and poetic experience. We have come close to that depth of being where consciousness becomes aware of 'its own voice', emerging from a reality in which vision and hearing are not subject to intellectual but to contemplative reasoning. We have also pointed out a gap between the perception of reality and the possibility of its verbal expression – the most profound difference between the attitude and function of the mystic and that of the poet.

The mystic stays silent and acts because he feels the impotence of words, or rather the obstacle that words set in the way of the experience of God; the poet, profound as he may be, and close to mystical animation, feels his limits and speaks nevertheless, feeling his mission to be bearing witness, as a guide for those who live within convention, or, outside convention, trying to understand and understand each other.

We are dealing with two types of individuality: the mystic arrives at perception through grace and ascetic practice, the poet through grace and verbal practice. Dante writes in his letter to Can Grande della Scala: "I wrote the *Comedia* for the sake of mankind". The theologian Hamar states:

> It is beyond compare easier to love while staying silent than speaking. The preoccupation with searching for words greatly impedes the feeling of the heart, which in that way loses something, if the loss is not compensated by the profit that others derive from it.

After this brief look at the interior of poetry, we may try a comparison with the exterior, aware that it is a single movement, that the internal and external world of a man are interdependent, as Schopenhauer says, since one cannot confront objectivity without the Kantian *a priori* of subjectivity. We speak of the 'external world' only through necessity of communication, since, as Hölderlin wrote, "man lives poetically". So we compare the 'making of poetry' with one of the most eminent aspects of every religious doctrine: to offer an image and order of the world accessible to all. At the base of every religion is the dogma of the divine unity of the world, the image of the world as a mirror of man and God.

But man tends, through convention, to impose an image of the world – no longer archetypal and divine, but one of ideologies and subjective projections. There is thus in society a cyclical recurrence of chaos, a repetition of ideological schemes that change with the changing of awareness and knowledge, schemes that manifest themselves, according to the forces current at the time, in movements of conservatism or of anarchy.

Poetry and art represent the ceaseless call to direct confrontation with the order of the world. Heidegger described this function of the poet:

> The poet summons to the song of his words all the clarity of the aspects of the heavens, all the sounds of his feelings and of his experiences, and so brings 'that which he summons' to shine and resonate.
>
> But the poet, if he is a true poet, does not describe the pure and simple appearance of the sky and the earth. The poet, in his view of the sky and of the earth, summons that which in its revealing of itself discloses that which is hidden, and how much is hidden ...

So the poet rediscovers the world every time, representing it through an intuition of a unity and an order and a measure within it, as Dante knew:

> O grace abounding, whereby I presumed
> to fix upon the eternal light my gaze
> so deep, that in it I my sight consumed! ...

But "to fix upon the eternal light my gaze" remains the impulse of every man who has the humility and the desire to 'look' at the world, and simultaneously feels the emotion of 'rediscovering it'. This is the impulse that manifests itself through love. As Leopardi said:

> Who does not speak
> Of your mysterious nature?
> Who has not felt
> your power among us?
> Yet always in telling of your effects
> the feeling itself spurs human tongues ...

In this force and in this concept lies the secret source of poetry.

We pass among trees and animals, between days and nights, in this great theatre of abysses and distances, of stars and heavens, and we meet with human beings, and we despair before the silence of stones and the threat of death. But none of all this is immanent to us, becoming ours, making itself close and miraculously true and existent in our hearts, except when the child and the poet reproduce it, or when we are affected by "the clear, fresh water", or by "the whispering moon" and "the sounding sea" or by the terrors of human-kind or the most gentle sweetness.

Petrarch, Leopardi, Virgil and Dante call us into wakefulness and to attention, they reveal the world and make it reality. The history of man would not have existed, or we would have no memory of it, if it were not for the testimony of the great poets. The poet presents a picture of the world that is a unity of the clear and the hidden; what it has become necessary to say and what cannot be told but is alluded to; what is thought and what emotion, what is ephemeral in form but eternal in substance, however much it may constantly change and evolve.

Perhaps this is why Goethe makes the chorus of *Faust* say:

> Sacred poetry ascend to heaven!
> And be like the splendid star,
> your light that spreads

further and yet further!
Yet it reaches us,
always and again where we hear
its beloved word.

Maritain approaches the status of poet when he speaks of "making himself Adam" in order to understand the world. Not permanently. One cannot leave out of consideration history, memory, the senses, education, moments of sleep, the frictions of the material world and its burdens (which drag their weight from all directions, *half way through life's journey*), everything that one can sum up as 'original sin'. But it is also true, as Cvetaeva has said, that "the poet attempts the impossible", "since I was born outside of time ..."

But it is precisely because of this devotion to a presumed innocence and originalness of the world, to the mystery of unexpected relationship with the word, that man awaits the miracle of poetry.

And do not think that all that we have up to now struggled to delineate represents a poetic itinerary, a literary theory. Nothing could be more wrong. It is what happens. The poet limits himself to gathering within himself and in words all that which life and grace have prepared for him. The poet and poetry, can only draw strength and rejuvenation from the liberty and abandonment of his own 'making' of poetry.

I have tried to reflect on the poetic driving force and its links between the word and mysticism, and would like to suggest a function of poetry in the contemporary world. The poetry of man makes the world in the image of God and harmony, just as violence makes it in the image of pride. This is not a confessional God but a God present even in his negation, who, as Karl Barth says, "is found even in our indifference", the God we face every time that "there is no difference between liberty and necessity", aware that "idolatry is to wish that God should correspond to our reason".

The God of the poet does not present himself through the suggestion and determination of the mind, just as the order of the world of the poet will not be subject to intellectual intention. Poetry is a real event. Even if the preparation for composition and drafting and re-drafting constitute a necessary preparation for the creation of poetry. As our great poet says:

Ma nondimen, rimossa ogne menzogna,
Tutta tua vision fa manifesta ...

It seems that we ourselves and the world are as one, that the image or vision is much closer than the distance separating it from our eyes, that in the instant the thing speaks to us, the world speaks to us. In that instant we are spectators of an eternal miracle: the relationship between our individuality and the life-force. The word of poetry has this force, this clarity, this sense of the unexpected. Delio Tessa wrote, in Milanese dialect:

... dilla ... redilla	... say it ... say it again ...
quella parola li,	that word,
e peu tornela a di	and then go back and say it again
e allora ... te comincet	and then it starts to be clear to you ...
a s'ciariss ... a capi ...	and you understand ...

bolla d'aria nell'aria	air bubble in the air
parola solitaria …	solitary word …

This clarity of understanding lasts only for the moment of the poetry, just as the force of the apparition lasts only for the moment of seeing. But then something will remain within us, and perhaps something will remain also in the memory, and the body and the psyche. Perhaps it will be no more than an allusion or a suggestion that leads to inquiry or introspection – but something creative that will remain in the written word or the sounds or the images of art. Through these miracles and messages, humanity nourishes the communal sense of belonging and hope, a stronger sense of self and of others, the starting point of inquiry and purpose.

The world weighs heavily on man in its laws of death and violence, in the weight of dead philosophies, in deceptive appearances, in the lies of convention, man's inertia leading to the servitude of the body and the mind, to the passions and arrogance of the ephemeral will of the ego. But poetry calls to movement, to the rediscovery of self, to evolutionary action, to hope. "No-one can love the dried-up husk …" wrote Goethe, however:

> That writing was written for me
> that did not show to everyone its sacred meaning …
> Its form mysteriously entranced me!

It is as if beauty may be the last veil, the tangible veil of the invisible truth, its shadow, but a shadow that moves in the light.

The poet gives a cosmic valancy to things, moving things to contemplation. The world is full of voices that invite man outside the solitariness of the body, that call individuals to solidarity with all and to the sacredness of people. As Zanzotto splendidly writes, in a bitter, agonised invocation:

> Should the darkness grow …
> one by one should the trees
> and branches and leaves of darkness
> grow darker
> should we all give birth in the dark …

Ecclesiastes admonishes: "all words are inadequate, no-one can describe everything …"; the poet can only evoke silence and darkness, things that seem silent yet having life, that seem in shadow yet awaiting the light:

> … the eye is not sated with seeing
> nor the ear overflowing with what it hears …

Religion and poetry-making (*poieo*) are going in the same direction: religion enjoining man to live a life of sanctity, to the practice of drawing nearer to the divinity; *poieo* charges them with speaking, with representing, with guiding themselves and other men towards the divinity, poetry.

In saying this, I am aware of going against the tide, restating once again a function of the poet and the artist, of poetry and art. Otherwise, one cannot see why literature should survive. As von Balthasar says:

> If beauty becomes a form that cannot be considered identical with being, with spirit and with liberty, then we are plunged in an epoch of mere aestheticism, and the realists are absolutely right to be hostile to beauty.

Composition *(1959), William Johnstone – artist's estate*

Composition (Northern Gothic) *(c1962), W J – Private Collection*

Thorbjørn Campbell

Blackwaterfoot Banshee

The plate-glass door reflects the empty fields;
the day is bright and white and light and lone;
the old receptionist sleeps at her desk
oblivious of the disembodied moan

that rises from the patio entrance side
where Mrs Winckelmann, all painted toes
and peeling skin, relaxes with a drink
as the thin woodwind sound around her grows.

Out in the cool stone store a kitchen boy,
middle-aged, weak-eyed, with short sandy hair,
hears it, but thinks of rain, damp hillsides and,
from youth, a far-off cliffside cottage where

the box-bed sleeper turned, flung out her arm
and sighed in answer to the long-drawn notes
that sounded in the huge old chimney-piece
and stirred among dark ashes orange motes –

and where, under an angry sky, he later
watched from the door an ambulance speed away
white in one strong stray gleam of sun, while rain
cascaded on himself, to fears a prey.

Since then, his mind's had only stillborn thoughts
whirling around in grey cyclonic limbus;
he can't make up his mind whether to shun
or to embrace the glory of a nimbus …

The wind quivers and elongates its note;
the sheep-grass ripples on the open hill.
Warmth toasts the thirsty Mrs Winckelmann.
The sky is parching, blue and heartless still.

Impassively he locks the storehouse door.
Give me more tears, he thinks, *more gusty sorrow.*
He tells the woman, "Make the most of it;
perhaps this wind means cloud and rain tomorrow."

Brent Hodgson

Proverbs of the 21st Century

Science:

1. Kill not the genetically modified goose that lays the golden egg.
2. The genetically modified donkey has a sting in its tail
3. The genetically modified child will eat wood as well as the paint on picket fences.
4. The genetically modified bloodhound who is idle recites Shakespearian sonnets to his fleas, but he that is hunting gives a running commentary
5. The genetically modified snail that will not carry a saddle, must have no oats
6. The genetically modified billy goat strikes with both hands.
7. The genetically modified donkey of six legs moves in mysterious ways.
8. Genetically modified blood is one colour – next year it shall be green
9. No man fears what he sows – unless it was genetically modified seed
10. Genetically modified dogs wag their four tails, not so much as in love as to send signals in semaphore.
11. The genetically modified goat must browse – when on the internet.
12. The genetically modified golden eagle breeds pink doves.
13. To fright a genetically modified mouse of five tonnes – is not the way to catch her.
14. The genetically modified man of sticky tongue catches more flies than vinegar.
15. The genetically modified cat has ninety-nine lives.
16. Why buy a genetically modified canary when milk is so cheap?
17. When genetically modified bees are old they yield no corn flakes.
18. All are good genetically modified fishes – but where do the fifty-foot long sprats come from?
19. You can lead a genetically modified dolphin to water – but you can not make him sink.
20. The genetically modified five-tonne mouse that can sing and *won't* sing, must be made to stop sitting on roof tops.
21. Never trust a genetically modified woman, even if she has borne you seven gold-egg laying geese.
22. He who has a genetically modified snake by the beard – has a hell of a time.
23. When the genetically modified polar bear is black and has no limbs – the French will still not love the English.
24. If the third eye of a Portuguese woman is coloured blue – the genetic-modifying scientist has made a mistake.
25. Whin by whin, the genetically modified Montrose man fills his belly.
26. He who rides the genetically modified tiger is bound to win at Ascot.
27. The best genetically modified Friesian cows of Dumfriesshire – swim near the bottom of the pond.

28. Let every genetically modified sheep – hang by his trunk.

29. Genetically modified butterflies seek poor men for their stomach; rich men stomach their shooting down.

30. Good riding at two saddles, men on the back of the genetically modified snail have told, for if one break, the other will hold.

31. How can the novo-farmer sleep soundly – when his genetically modified pigs are ripe?

32. It is too late to shut the gates of the zoo – after the genetically modified tortoise has flown away.

33. The duck that drinks not wine after salad, is in danger of being genetically re-modified

34. Genetically modified human legs that are too highly stretched, either soon snap or quickly go out of tune.

35. He that has both of his hands in the mouth of a genetically modified guinea pig – must make his will as best he can.

Women:

1. It is easy to be wise – after your wife has spoken to you.

2. If you sell your wife to your best friend – make sure give **him** her DIY tools, steel-capped safety boots and blue overalls.

Sex:

I. There is only one good skin-tight blue lurex dress in the country – and every cross-dressing man swears it is in his wardrobe

2. There is only one good skin-tight blue lurex dress in the country and you're not getting it – it's mine.

Men:

I. No fat man is an island – unless he is floating in the sea.

Robots:

I. The sharper the tin snips, the sooner the old robot turns over.

2. The hungry robot in time may bite in two the kitchen table.

3. The bad robot always blames his maker.

4. For want of a screw, the foot was lost;/ for want of a foot; the robotic butler was lost;/ for want of a robotic butler, the candle-lit diner was lost.

5. The gods send Boots No 7 lipstick and face powder to those who have metallic bodies.

Wisdom:

1. You can not teach a computer nerd to lay new bricks.

2. No man can change a white sheet into the colours of the rainbow – unless he is a house-husband doing the laundry.

3. Spanners maketh the farm boy into the head of a multi-national automobile company (viz. Henry Ford).

4. Dogs who live in glass houses should not throw bones.

5. Coarse sand does not make a DESSERT – unless you live in Arizona.

6. It is an ill submariner that sinks under the dinner table.

7. There was never a good town but had a radio-active dump at one end.

8. The proof of the pudding is in the stepping-in of it.

9.   Spin doctoring is unprofitable to them that never tried it.
10.   Lock your door that ye may make your neebor get oot his sledge hammer.
11.   Triple chceseburgers are good for nocht but shade.
12.   If those on Zimmer frames lead others on Zimmer frames – all shall fall into the sheuch.
13.   He that ceases to haiver – will never become a Scottish poet.
14.   A leaping Rottweiller with nae teeth gives nae headache
15.   A leaping Rottweiller with teeth is never a Good Dog Year.
16. Being charitable to the wee man from the Save the Sparrows of the World Society, is better than having your windies put in
17. When a businessman is tired of London – he can always retire to Plockton.
18.   Fat arse sits in the parlour when the loon is kicked oot the door
19.   If you deal with a modem architect – think of his Lego bricks.
20.   Thrie things never to be trusted: a spin doctor, a spin doctor and a spin doctor.
21.   Never swear in the presence of farmyard ducks – they might be God-fearing Quackers.
22.   Thc bread is always greener on the other side of the supermarket aisle.
23.   He who sneezes at the beginning of the First Movement – picks up the conductor's baton.
24.   Imitation butter is mad every day of the year.
25.   The red cow gives milk – to the proletariat.
26.   He that eats the king's goose feather mattress – will choke to death.
27.   Better bend – than incur the wrath of the pricst.
28.   Nae mischief – but a priest at the altar hoy's bottom.
29.   The mair mischief – the better the altar boy's bottom.
30.   Misfortune makes Lord Archer a friend of the prison warden.
31.   Whan the Tartan Army is led by a pride of lions
– very disastrous will it be for any Scottish player who runs oot of puff.
32.   Never open the door to a wee man from the Save the Sparrows of the World Society – lest a big man enter along with him.
33.   If you go head-butting on the Sunday, the polis will come to assist you
34.   It is a short High Street that has nae handbag snatchers
35.   The ladder is a world – for the window cleaner to fall off.
36.   The arboriculturist that loves Marks & Spencer, loves all the branches.
37.   Cast a moggie over your hoose – and you'll be reported to the RSPCA.
38.   Oot of the causey into the radio-active Solway Firth with its nutrient-rich sewage and fertiliser run-off residue.
39.   A field of ripe wheat requires thrie things: a combine harvester, a computer and an Information Technologist installed in the combine's cab.
40.   The train journey from Edinburgh to Carlisle through the Borders is aye marred – by the lack of a railway track.
41. Wise words on the anticipation of living a long life: The missile with the nuclear warhead seldom explodes twice.

Donald Smith

from the poem sequence 'Airthra'

One

Fire in the agate
bubbling lava veining quartz
mica flaking
Schist Uchil hard watcher of the folding sandstone
settled layers ice sculpted
sedimenting water soils seeding trees and ferns
bog mosses, rushes, the river slowly flows through

Three

Seven swans
white necks outstretched,
geese thirteen sounding southwards from the ice
two herons poise stilted on the firth.
One hovering kestrel
and the long upwind water winds gently
to the hard blue salt chopping race
north crested Sea.

Eye sweeps Eagle cruises
Uchil Range Campsie Fells
Barrier of Bannog
to the distant sun-reflecting bens.
Scatter of deer on Drumnach ridge
rising from the marsh,
wood-spread shelters squirrel and fox,
beaver otter badger bear.
Wolves stake north
running reindeer red pull down
the wild white bull winter-weakened,
wary of the seven pointer Stag
belling in the spring.

Four

Two hundred years on open plains
I lived a herd in shape of ox.

Three hundred years of covered canopy
wild boar of trees tusk master.

Five hundred years was still
an ancient form of bird
on heron's wings.

One thousand mottled years,
a silver salmon in the flood.

A fisher caught me in his net,
the woman dressed me lovingly

She ate alone
her belly swelled
and I slipped out a twisting snake.

Issue of woman I was born –
one hundred years
a bloomin man.

Five

Climbing upwards
zig-zag through the oaks
birch rowan furze and ash
fringe the burn's deep channel
cutting to the ridge.

Against the sky gawky fast,
gold clasped on white memoriser of the tribe
gateway to rebirth in training
hard druid discipline, absent youth.

Long legs stretch out along the hill towards the Dun.
Shifting on the slope
brown movement turns the eye.
Girl not deer. Watches.
She climbs steady to the brow.

He follows crossways to intersect her path
but crouches low,
hair tied back heading for the pool
to bathe in springtime
no splashing children but alone.

Turn back or track every coiling step.
Silent in the heather, gently fingers yellow broom
to see the low set water rushes edging rippled surface
in the cold clear blue and white hill air
lifting from the foot
the skin rolls up thigh hair, brown belly
shoulder white against the golden neck.

She wades into the pool
rushes part, arms screened across her breasts.
One swift opening, aureoles to the sun
elbows wide like wings she drops on the surface wake
the neck a prow pent up breath releasing.

He turns quickly back still unnoticed
homes to his mother's hearth.

Six

The black month comes, ice thickens,
lamps burn in shelters, sickness
hunger,
death moves free.

Sometimes the sky is hung with lights
above the mountain,
waits the narrow day.

First the preparation.
Water poured in stone
pure cold.

Second gathering embers from each hearth,
borne to the circle.

Third the tryst
of fire and water, sun and rain
in hissing union.

Fourth the washing:
water-carried to each house,
garments stripped
lustration.

Vigil fifth, a round of dark and light.
We fast inside
the chamber of the dead.

That night the Sun confirms
one lingering setting
down the passage.

Night Long Dread

Fire signals, torches flicker
light and water laid on stone
– a silver gleam

Sunrise through the pillars,
two mounds of stone warmed by life,
the golden throat will sound again.

Seven

I got up early and slipped away without breakfast.
Over the estate wall and up the tussocky field rabbits bobbing.
The dyke tumbled long ago topped now with stob and wire,
I once saw roebuck clear it in a single grace-powered bound.
Between the wires I go and in among a fringe of trees,
windbreak and storm shelter for the spread of loch and park.
I come out into light, rinsed in dew,
water in the shadow of the wooded hill,

trees dawn-leaved with mist.
I cut round the western end, rhododendrons shouting for the sun.
Double Dykes, Roman Cutting, Parkhead,
Highlandman's Well, the Devil's Turn to Logie.

I turn east instead along the shaded shore,
short cut on a summer morning, suddenly taut,
tugged by an absence, I start towards the Stone,
upright on the gentle brow twice my height untoppled.
Now I hear feet pound on the ground,
racing past the green, down the track.
Across barbed wire islanded with stalks of barley,
one last burst – the sandstone sentinel is in my arms
pressed sunwarm palms caress the weathered face
but cannot meet rough join sob-tearing now this other touch.

Without you husked chaff called out before I knew myself
this morning, chased for life.

Eight

He travels the drovers' way by Blackford and Dunblane
up onto the muir and down again at Logie.
Clouds becalm windless air,
feet sore and itchy whirr of flies, bees buzz,
grass dried thistledown drifting. The staff slows its strike
at Highlandman's well a trickle
barely dampens tongue and lips.
The last twisting drop to Logie by the Devil's Turn.
Through leafy shade the cleft smooths out
green pasture by a bubbling burn,
a welcome hut in sheltered grove.
Touch of water tingling on the feet,
a hirpling canopy of light and shade
no flash of swift or swallow, the lull a humming solitude
the saintly Serf slips into sleep.

Green island off the shore sea birds solitary call
the white foam breaks on sandy beach
upborne a floating coracle in silver stream of fish
a maiden's naked form
alabaster numb chastened by the sea.
Lift her gently in the sealskin
broken on a chariot's axle thrown down the rock face
a king set fast against her vows rapes her dream of holiness,
a baby in her womb, complete and fragile,
cast adrift into the estuary the sacred cargo comes,
guided by the waves around a blessed circling isle.
Lower her softly by the ashes
healing warmth gives life and movement to the limbs

while in the watery globe a pulse begins to beat
stirring for the gates of birth,
tugged and pulled towards the light.

Dreaming Kentigern,
here in the druid grove
Saint Serf will plant his Shepherd's crook.

Nine

Early morning on the hill climbing past Parkhead
a surge of sheep burst over Fossachie,
break on the rocky crest a wash of grey on green
bleating wildly bunching gaggle-bound to a reluctant front.
Till over come the dogs racing round untidy edges
whistling sweep of stragglers in the bobbing flotsam.
I swing the outer gate and let the tide flow in.

The shepherd follows last and pulls the gate behind,
crook on arm content to see them fanked heaving backs and rumps cool,
standing time for thick strong tea and smoke.

I set up the platform winding cable round the pole,
unroll woolsacks stacking blades in boxes,
prising cans of buist and scrape irons clean.

Jera, Drumbrae, Pendreich and Fossachie himself they come,
quiet men before a long day's shearing.
The sun warms to its task
but before the buzzing scrape of shears I listen to the rising dew
broken only by the baa of lambs and breath of black-nosed yows,
brown eyes wait to be shorn quivering to break loose,
sprung free of winter's weight a pure white stream in spate
migrating to the mountain pasture
till driven down in autumn speaned and culled
to face another winter.

Eleven

On an afternoon of slate grey skies, cracked ice underfoot
I took the sheltered back road
Hermitage Wood to Logie.
Flurries of snow-packed clouds
refused to give the comfort of a fall,
bone trees ribbed above the track tensed northwards on the slope.

What kind of hermit lived up there,
a cell beneath the cliff and steps cut into the rock?
He could survey the Forth
or walk along the Carlie Craig where high above the kirk
women by ordeal were cast down to the Devil.
More like a Laird's notion,

hermit wanted for a final touch
to his wild ordered fashion.

He stepped back to admire and tumbled down the steps.
Tales of an unlucky breed, young heirs repeatedly drown
dropping through black icy holes that shiver on old fault lines.

Swing on halfway to Logie when freeze stock still
the seven-pointer guards the crossroads,
head erect, nose twitching at the scent,
his chest held high on stilts the winter king in exile.
Liquid eyes long gaze of time
he turns canters off into the wood
through which he came foraging into the yards.
I follow his old memory into the ruins of a farm,
eyeless cottages where children played,
cobbled barns and tumbled byres.
Their people died in some great freeze,
migrated to a warmer land or drifted
leaving mouldered ruins to remember.

The stag and I stand witness.
They walked like me to Logie where crowstepped gable
surmounted by an empty belfry through which the snow squalls
stands sentinel on tumbling seas of stone,
scythes and skulls, the mason's square,
an hour glass and winged angels.
Voices blown round roofless walls
or the wind's own sterile breath.

Fifteen

Wheel high on curve of cloud and sun
airborne in the current flow to the mountain
across a dappled loch
through groves of trees soft turning on the wind,
oak elm ash
and sheen of silver birch leaves
nod delicately between the rocks
rivulets of deer step to the hill in coats of autumn red,
heads held high bear time's insignia.
People raise their narrow beds,
toppling death's dark scythemen,
stones crack apart,
grains run from the hourglass to join the washing stream.
Mould and lichen memory leave in body of light
earth rises to greet the revenants. I not-I
You, not-you
in death in life forever.
Airthra.

Last Tango in Glasgow

Jack Withers

Quite depressing. Out there the heavens hung heavy and he felt as if he could soon go a real bevvy. But no, that was *not* how to try and escape from his ain Glasgow ghetto, for if you're intent on trying to win you've gotta learn how to open up and not to stun.

Ay, Glasgow. Primitive wild child and ah kennt his faither but no Kentigern. Hello? Hello? Is this Glasgow? Speaking. Listening. Sweating. Germinating. Vegetating. Out of control. No will? No soul? No goal?

When one exists alone is the telephone a good thing or not? When all you've got is your labour tae sell yiv got tae watch not to be easily bought in big capital's juggernaut, bad enough as it is wi this omnipresent stink of baith dry and wet rot, in a rut and caught like an itinerant ant in a sweet treacle-pot.

So he went tae the window and hud a shufti doon oan Glasgow: cops, shops, cars and skyscrapers. Vista panoramic and paranoiac. Thick sick traffic and everywhere intruders, muggers, pushers, no-hopers, dossers and thou-shalt-not passers. Crime marches on. To oblivion, annihilation, extinction? A last throw of the dice alang the slippery ice? So where's that button? And no tae forget tae take yir pick.

Oh tae be a genius and no jist anither joker or bum-actor who couldnae quite get his act thegither.

Somehow he'd lost his equilibrium and felt as if he was trapped in a vacuum wheezing and sneezing wae the snotters blinding him. Go then and see yir GP? No way, as it wis the symptom that wis the problem and no the disease, sae sneeze, sneeze, sneeze and get up aff yir knees.

Fair enough. Or wis it? As the thinker noo thinks that he's sumthin special noo that he's no longer an out-patient attending the mental hospital. On the ither hand his mind takes note and feeds on the self-deception as always between and beyond the lies the surprise of the ultimate fusion of guess and illusion that leads tae some kind of conclusion.

One must admit here that trying tae make sense of existence is one intense exercise which may or may not reveal the essence and ethereal presence of what lies behind those deluded and hooded eyes, for a Glasgow schizo just has tae know itherwise the soul dies. To be a catalyst and not exist in a mindless mist is vital for his spiritual well-being as they say in Springburn. "I may be lost but somehow I shall return," which was quite a mouthful coming from him.

He needs and even demands silence for each poetry-reading, does the thinker. As long as there is an audience, that is, so that he can exploit each and every pause and nuance, in order to rejoice in the music of his own voice, each word being an integral chord and sharp sword just like some square-go Glasgow oratorio. What? Poet of the proletariat? Nuthin better than that. Or?

The folk are dead sick and shallow and narrow. Conditioned the minds, heavy are the blinds. How tae react tae this unsigned fact seen on a cludgie-wall?

Knock-knock.

Who's there?

Monty.

Monty who?

'Mon tae fuck.

He was forced tae laugh as humour's truly a funny thing, no doubt about that, particularly in this dark atrocity of a big city. "Cut the chat ya wee rat or else ah'll batter ye roon the flat wae ma second-haun baseball bat." What crudity and depravity plus the anonymity. The Social Security. Screws oan the loose oot yonder in Easterhoose. "Did ye poke her, ya wee joker, or did ye hit her wae the poker, merr's like it, eh?" Ay, and in for the kill in Blackhill wae yir heid oan the block in Pollock. Blood in the mud and spit oan the concrete. Should blacks get the Fair Holiday? Dead crude and real rude. Kill yirsel laughin? Ay, mebbe ye should.

The thinker recognises the need for structure, baith inner and outer, itherwise one goes shapeless and clueless intae yon concrete wilderness. The desperate need is there for an all-round architecture for the future. One that eliminates all waste and excess. But how then to hold it all together including the centre?

Silence. He may as well talk to the wall and so he does. "It's a perverse universe," he says. Prays? No, says.

Without a goal we're all shooting into one huge black hole. That's for sure. Or is it? A pit is more like it. Ay, a bottomless pit. One without coal?

Were there bibles on the tables that Christ upset?

The thoughts were all there, but how to string them all together and make them mean something even though something is missing everywhere, including the human condition? Quite. Quite a question. One that will lead to self-destruction and annihilation? We'll see. Or will we?

Like life, a short story should have a beginning, a middle and an end otherwise you can end up going out of your mind or round the bend. Whatever.

And now you can buy a cheap copy of the New Testament down yonder in the bargain-basement. Yet anither sign that disaster is imminent?

He suddenly remembers how he danced his last tango in the Glasgow Locarno learned from watching the sensuous craft of George Raft up on the cinema-screen in the film *Floating Timbers*. In *pampas* tempo. Don't die for me Erchie and Tina. His partner? Mary or Betty wae visions o' cake and confetti? Can't remember and, anyway, it disnae matter.

He looks around at all his books. Masses of them, so why the sudden odium? At least maist huv spines and are not nervous wrecks and, of course, are sources of wisdom. Hidden? No, open to anyone who can read and think, and then go on to build a New Jerusalem. Hallelujah!

Scotland. Sin-land on Sunday. Out of mind and underhand with nothing planned other than an unreal reel played by a second-hand ceilidh-band. Scotland benighted.

Ay, science has no conscience, no instintive intuition, no *tabula rasa* for the human condition. Deep down could even be classed as being inhuman. So provide an end-solution? Press button. Armageddon.

Longings and shortcomings? Life in the raw and without the trimmings.

a) A blood-red star descends on an inhuman abattoir
b) An imminent end to a distant parliament
c) The inability to walk on air and eliminate fear
d) To see and be by a frozen sea sailing on into infinity
e) To return, begin and start again
f) Reach maturity before you're ninety
g) Unable tae write the great Scottish novel
h) To climb the hill and not the wall
i) Big in vision but deficient in talent
j) To understand the mind's no man's land
k) No meaning to anything

As a thinker he should know better but doesn't. Interaction and sharing with others is relevant and equally important. To get out and about more rather than this continuous self-examination and going over the score again and again like some insane composer. To try and grasp the banality of everyday reality. To interact and suffer and join in the frivolity. To go for long walks along the Clyde and down by the docks. To get out and away from the big city.

Yet anither rejection doesn't help his depression one bit or even a lot. Vomit. Out the window and all over Glasgow? Sure, why not? Sudden disgust and a need to get pissed.

I am.
I think.
I'm parched.
Drink.
Before or after?
Never.
Liar.

There seems to be no retreat from a planet of plastic and solid concrete. Been down tae the shops and avoided the cops.

Why? A nerve twitches in his eye. Done nothing so why does he feel so guilty about something? Much more altruistic than calvinistic he is. A case for analysis? He punctures the can and drinks like a man. Or even like a woman. *Vive la difference* or an act of conscience?

Mary-Anne fill my can, for your honour John Riley is dry, so am I.

Out on the horizon a skyscraper is burning like a mountain of paper. Yet another arsonist or even terrorist. Wait till they install water-meters and common heaters. Mass protest? Fire-brigades storming the barricades? Eliminate the rodents swarming in the basements? Weed out the militants?

Cleanse the housing-schemes and destroy revolutionary dreams? Calm the blood and nip any Trotskyist act in the bud? Workers of the world take fright? Cripple those archangels and any remaining disciples of Marx and Engels? Red sky over Ruchazie the dark pierced by a glowing arc? Counter yon big mean machine? The thinker took a shower as he felt unclean.

Finding the going tougher than ever, the big question being is man's natural condition to be soldier and killer in the heat of war? How we can't police and manage the peace. How we act through fear. The restlessness. The uneasiness. The stress. The disease of big business. The underlying lying with nothing ever culminating in something clear and illuminating.

SOS.

Mayday! Mayday!

Christ we're lost.

Why did we ignore our bloody past?

The bills keep coming.

Those voices keep on returning.

Hear them, hear them?

Can't cope.

The rent is imminent.

Out of his element.

Everything is oscillating.

Suffocating.

Footsteps out in the corridor.

Horror.

Think. Act. Do something. Think again. Heart hammering. Asthmatic breathing. Alarming. All in vain. Too late to take a shot of cocaine. Inner confusion. No decision. Knock-knock. Paranoiac. Quick. Feels sick. Close to midnight. Too late to turn out the light. Should have taken to the hills away from those mountains of bills. Love thy neighbour and thy brother. Square cell. Twelfth floor. Tomb of a room. Dumb in this modern slum.

Sudden cracks building towards some kind of climax. Poll-tax? Rodin or Desperate Dan. Elbow on knee and hand on chin. Power of reflection. But action? Last question before he hit the deck or rather the tarmac. Deranged and unhinged. Diabetic and schizophrenic. Nervous wreck. Loner and outsider. Dissident? No comment. Who's to blame?

No one in our opinion as the ambulance left in silence.

Back to *Das Kapital* in Gartnavel Hospital.

But elemental not sentimental.

Jack Withers

Clever Bombs

Clever bombs clever bombs
how smart you are
you've passed your exams
and are now itching for war

Yes clever bombs clever bombs
you've got your degree
for you killing may be thrilling
but certainly not for me

Clever bombs clever bombs

you've studied hard and done your sums
and love to see things go up in flames
good old friend
old buddies and bodies right on to the end

Caramba

Without even so much as a warning
one peaceful night
the combined might

of Cuba, Grenada and Nicaragua
invaded and occupied
the USA.

Caramba!

Just like that at the drop of a hat
Reds sailed into the film-set
and what had constituted
the real free world
had been destroyed
in the stench and smoke
of so much burning celluloid.

So let us hope and pray
that come the end of the day
God will bless and save
America
and for that matter
Europe and Asia.

We have been warned.

David C Purdie

Bricks

For my wife on her retirement

When I was young and you were beautiful,
we built our life with days. Our days were bricks.
Our bricks were made with the clay of minutes,
and the straw of seconds.

At first we were building in an open field,
without shelter from the wind that strove
to level the bricks, and sink our efforts in the mud.

And each brick took eternity
to mix, and form, and set in place – we thought
the building would never, ever, end.

But now I'm old and you are beautiful,
we make and build our bricks in no time.
Our days have turned into years,
and, if walls have ears, our years
are walls.

The walls give shelter from the gusts of life
within them, we can huddle together, warm and safe.

I love the walls we've built with all
the bricks of our days.

The Nature of the Malt

The nature of the malt
was built from snow thawed slow in gullies:
that trickled over barren stone,
and melted into peatbogs:
that oozed from springs,
joined forces with hill burns;
digesting soil, heather, bracken,
gathering elements of every kind,
copper, iron, silver and gold.

The barley was blown
by clean sweet airs,
it swelled in fields,
feeding on nitrogen,
and drinking the rain and haar.

It heard the voices
of the labourers in the fields;
the speak of the workers

who turned the barley malt;
and took on something of their ways –
dryness, austerity,
and hidden warmth.

With peat flame and steam,
the distillers worked their alchemy,
once – then once again,
turning base ingredients into gold.

Time took over –
deep inside the barrel's belly,
the spirit breathed in
the fragrance of oak and sherry.

The cask kept the unhatched whisky safe,
ripening in its womb,
until the birthing time.

Pour it always with respect;
sip slow and contemplate its complexity.
The dram will reward you –
for that is the nature of the malt.

Reality

What I see is not you,
only light reflected
from your hair, your clothes, your skin.

But, when I see you,
you are made of sun,
that radiates from you and lights my way.

What I hear is not you,
only air vibrating,
on a scrap of skin inside my ear.

But, when I hear you,
you are made of music,
that echoes in my soul, and thrills me through.

And when I touch you,
are you really real –
though you are warm as sunlight,
and melodious as the music of the spheres?

Only when you surround me,
and we move together:
when we drink each other's breath,
and our bodies melt into one –

only then, you are reality.

Ettlins

An owersettin o the Desiderata bi Max Ehrmann

Gang lown amang the dirdum an the grush, an mind whit pace there aiblins is in seelence. Sae faur as ye can, athoot renoonce, be on guid tairms wi ilka bodie. Spick yer sooth quatelike and clair an tak tent o ithers, ein the duil an unkennin haes their tale an aa. Eveit lood an rammish fowks, they ir deavin til the speirit. Gin ye even yersel wi ithers ye'll aiblins get vauntie-like or soor kis there will aye be gryter an lesser fowk nor yersel. Tak pleisure whan ye bear the gree an in yer schames forby. Tak tent o yer troke for, hooivver hummil it micht be, it is a haddin amang the chyngin fortouns o time. Be tentie in yer daeins kis the warld is fu o swickerie, but dinna lat it blin ye tae whit guidness there is. Fu mony a chiel is eydent tae be gracie; an ivverygait life is fu o smeddum. Be yersel. Maistlie, dinna pit on fainness, nor be ye ware o luve for it is, in maugre o hert-scaud an scunner, as ayelestand as the girse. Tak bienlie the coonsel o the years an mensfulie renoonce the graith o youthheid. Fess up strenth o speirit tae beild yersel in sidden mishanter, but dinna fash yersel wi ill jalousin – muckle dree is brocht aboot wi tire an lanesomeness. Ayont a halesome discipleen, caa canny wi yer ainsel. Ye ir a bairn o the universe nae less nor the trees an the starns, ye hae a richt tae bide here. An whuther or no it's clair til you, athoot doot the univairse is unfauldin as it suid dae. Sae he douce wi God, whitivver ye trew Him til be. An nae maitter whit yer darg an yer howps is, amang the breeshle o life, bide at pace wi yer sowel. Wi aa its sconcin an brucken drames it is aye an on a bonny yird. Be cantie. Ettle tae be blithe.

Dauvit Horsbroch

Ootrel Innin

The stounin comes fae furth the Yird
we ken we'r no oor lane
seignals sent lik haly wurd
gar naitions mak the mane

Frichtit fowk that haes the say
for wappons stairt tae deek
feart for some galactic ray
that Yirdlins comes tae seek

The faithers o releigion gang
awa tae hear the thing
an if whit's true is richtlie wrang
oor faiths wull tak the ding

But ae thing that micht be rare
is oor warld comes thegither
o weirs on Yird we hae nae mair
tae fecht oor Ootrel brither

Aidom's Aipple

Frankenstein he's faur fae deid
as Antinori daws
wheechin aipples fae the brainch
an gauin joco saws
– tae fesh anither Aidom

Frankenstein he's tae the fore
sae frichtnin shaws
makkin marras oot o men
bi brekin moral laws
– tae rear anither Aidom

Frankenstein he's feart o nane
deif til ither caws
hairstin louns fae deid grun
an plouin human raws
– tae grow anither Aidom

Frankenstein he's lowse o God
whyle argie-bargie jaws
gangin dooble-laddies kythe
wi seedless baws
– a prattic cruel on Aidom

The Derry Jig

Ower the sheuch thay dae an auld style jig
whan thousans o neds stairts actin the pig
the'r nae need o pairtners or fouterie steps
juist fire an stanes an bottles o meths

In Derry thay dae it wi a style aw thair lane
whan flutes stairt playin the toun's gien tae flame
sae ingangs the RUC tae cut throu the thrang
turnin the dancers fae fashous tae bang

In peinies an sashes wrocht fae orange an green
journeyman bigots jyne the waltz tae be seen
thae papists an prodies wi secterian creed
gang jiggin thair gait on the bing o the deid

At the Ceilidh

Iain Crichton Smith

Translated from the Gaelic by Kevin MacNeil

I met her last night at a ceilidh. I didn't recognise her, but I was told who she was. She was … she was … *ugly*. Her face had closed strangely in on itself like a purse.

She wasn't the one I knew in my youth, was she?

She was in the same class as me at school, long years ago. Her face was fresh and radiant, her hair black; she was exquisite. I remember one time going after a turnip for her; at the time there was a garden behind the school. This was during the war.

I thought of her constantly, awake or asleep. I wanted to protect her from the world. Not that the world was bad at the time, though there was a war going on. Once, the schoolmaster threw a large book at her for falling asleep in his class. I almost jumped on him.

You were at a dance, he yelled.

Was it jealousy in his voice as his glasses flashed?

I also wrote poetry. In class I strove to make a fool of myself so that she would notice me. At the time I was reading the poetry of William Ross. Didn't he himself die because of a woman, too?

It is difficult to go back to those days. In my mind they are soaked in fragrance, the mornings are brighter than they ever were after that. I was as light as a feather. The world was eternal.

How could I join in the war, I thought. I could be a pilot swooping down from the sky, wiping out the Nazis. She would hear that I was a great hero. Or I would stand on the deck of a sinking ship, with all guns blazing.

There's nothing as pure as young love, as first love. It is without guilt; it is undefiled. It renews the earth, raising flowers from winter itself. The soul desires nothing but to sacrifice itself. When I go back to those days they are entirely different from the world in which I am alive now. And she's in this realm still.

Who is she, then? Is she the one I saw at the ceilidh or the one who was once in school with me? My heart rejects the notion that she is the one at the ceilidh. For certain, the two are at variance. The one I knew is more vivacious than the one I saw last night. Could I say to her, Where did the other one go? You are imitating the one that once existed. You're not her at all.

Would it be right to say that to her?

When you look at a picture of yourself that was taken when you were young, you don't recognise this boy or that girl at all. You don't remember much that happened to them. He was bold, you are wary, he was handsome, you are old. If you met him on the street, he would laugh. Look at that old fool, he would say. Who's he?

Dear Peggy, where did you go? What box are you in? Where did they put you? Are you a prisoner somewhere?

Your hair was so black, your eyes were as bright as the stars, you were like a ripening fruit. Many's the time you broke my heart. I picture you laughing in the Italian café we'd frequent. And again, I see you at university.

Just yesterday I was at a funeral and an image came back to me. It was a cold day and the sea, so grey and wild, was roaring. There was a brittle ice on the ground. The coffin lay in the hole. And your face came back to me again in the warmth of youth; I thought it was stronger than death itself. Your body, your skin, the fragrance around you. In your school skirt.

We leave one world for another world. But we're not the same people. The philosophers say we are, but I'm not so sure. The days put lines on our faces. We meet some people we once knew and we don't recognise them. We say to ourselves, That's not them at all. They say they knew us, but they didn't, they didn't.

I looked at you with horror last night. It wasn't you who was there at all, of that I'm certain. Those weren't your eyes, those weren't your cheeks. A fearsome power has got a hold of you. You were extinguished utterly.

O, you were dancing at the ceilidh right enough, you were making conversation, you were singing, you were laughing.

But it wasn't you, I'm sure of that. And I believe you thought the same thing about me. This bald man. Who's he, where did he come from? He is so quiet, he doesn't have a word to say.

Time itself kills us. And yet it doesn't. I must stick resolutely to this thought. The woman I saw last night, she was an imposter. As though the devil himself instead of an angel were on the same floor as I was.

Though you stretched out your hand to me, it wasn't you. I realised that when I looked in your eyes. There was distraction in them, and also aversion.

I see them still, that couple who were young. They are still alive. They are more alive than these two who are speaking to each other. It is not good for us to bother them. They are alive in a garden that will not perish. Is that what the story of Adam and Eve was saying? But I don't have any memory of the two who left the garden. Where did *they* go?

I'm telling you just now. I don't recognise you. You're not my girlfriend at all. What did you do to the other one, the one I knew? Did you kill her, did you do away with her in a certain way? Were you envious of her?

It occurred to me when I was young that you were too beautiful, that they would destroy you. And that's what they did. They placed you in a prison, just as the song says. I didn't understand that song until this very moment. They put walls around you, old bones, an old body. And you're trying to get free but you can't.

I know this because it happened to me. At times I try to get out of my prison, but the mirror before me is too strong. When I see certain moons, swimming from cave to cave in the sky, that boy comes out of his shell like a rare bird. He senses a new smell, a scent he once knew; the dewy field rises around him. But the sun ascends once more, sending him back to his cage.

I refute you. You are not her at all. Don't speak to me. Sit back in your chair. Listen to the music. But I know you're not her. She is together with me in another world.

The book sails through the room and hits you.

I see hair that has turned grey and a face that has withered.

But it's not you, it's not you at all.

You're nothing but an imposter, Mrs, in this music which I'm listening to and in which I don't hear your voice though you are sing along with the others in the hall.

She and He

There was no one in the meadow but the two of them – she and he – in the ineffable light that was pouring from the beginning of the world. The single apple shone like blood on the tree, as red as a rose, as polished as glass.

'I want the apple,' she said. Her eyes were as calm as an infant's eyes, as heaven itself. Dark angels fluttered within them.

'The apple doesn't belong to us,' he said, his eyes filled with thoughts of God, of freedom, of nature…

'I want the apple,' she said, her eyes drawing towards her the fruit that shone like a jewel in the air.

He turned away from her eyes and looked into the eyes of the animals, eyes that sparkled like water. He saw nothing in them except himself. But, in *her* eyes …

'Look,' he said, 'at how the trees grew and how they gave birth to that apple. Isn't it marvellous how the sun and the water and the stars contributed. Doesn't it amaze you, to see the harmony of the universe, like strings on a harp?'

'I want the apple,' she said. And he looked at her. There were dark angels in her eyes; he started trembling like a tree in a storm. He burned in the fire of her eyes. He saw her covering herself with leaves from the trees like green mist around the sun.

The stars went past in gold and silver and he saw her entwining them like handcuffs with her white hands until they had the form of a snake. He let out a cry but the world righted itself again: the glass didn't break. He raised his hands, stopped, and turned, but her eyes were like a fire on his face, burning through his bones like paper. He looked down; the leaves were about her. He plucked the apple from the tree and saw her teeth as white as innocence tearing the skin of the fruit.

Long years afterwards, he composed poetry about it.

The Countryside in Wartime, Broomhill *(c1923)*
William Johnstone – Private Collection

Fragments of Experience *(1979)*, *WJ – Hope Scott Collection, Edin. Uni.*

Martin Bates

Euphorbia in January

You know, flower, I've never had the mind
to look at you closely before
to gaze steadily into your small dark faces

under their conical hats of green
and to imagine I see intelligence
stirring within them.

We have no common language, that's for sure.
You have the wisdom of silence
come rain, hail, tempest or blaze of sun.

I am a chatterbox like most of us humans
but amid the chatter a truth-worm gleams
imagining in the emptiness

sympathetic conversations
in which I get through to others
and they to me.

So I do with you, flower,
imagining you holding your breath
and staring at my lips.

Country people give you a strange name
suggesting seed and desire – spurge.
But we will use the lingua franca of Linnaeus

and name you Euphorbia
after the physician to the King of Mauretania
according to my dictionary –

which says no more –
cumbersome word, far removed
from your slender, nodding reality.

I like your quietness, holding my gaze
this winter evening all alone
as Mozart scales his violin

nimbly over the rock face of my heart.
My eyes rest on your green intentness.
God is in the detail, someone said,

or was it the devil?
You are beautiful, I say,
if the word means anything to you.

Beautiful you are and – may I say –
a trifle cheeky at close quarters?
I see now your faces are not black

but deep indigo or purple
and from their centre they stick out
their creamy tongues at me.

Is that a pout I see among the green tassles –
a wink, a nod, a grin?
Hold on a bit or I'll soon be hearing you chortle.

I have placed you in the jug with the broken handle
When I cut you, you bled your sweet white poison blood
all along the clay tiles.

I placed you in the arms of your sister, Rosemary.
It is January but here in the south you are both in bloom.
Rosemary gleams with the pallor of starlight.

In my northern land all flowers are now clenched
tight against the freezing air
except for the snowdrop timorously stirring.

It is cold here too – bitter.
I burn olive prunings against the frost
to keep the flame alive

in this land of illusion
now when the north wind blows away
all but the most stubborn of dreams.

Mozart moves in serene frenzy
to the climax
fusing darkness and light.

I will shift soon but I will marvel still
at your beauty I have passed by
and your courage in opening to such bleak skies

knowing something
of the fullness of time
that I know nothing of.

A Bargain

Somewhere up there in the high sierra
I wrote a poem and lost my dark glasses.
Not a bad bargain.

Scrambling among rocks, dodging thorns
I must have shoved them high above my brow
better to observe the purple of irises

so when I ducked beneath a burnt out pine
they must have gone flying.
And my poem – will it also go flying?

It was a lonely place
but I like to think a shepherd's green eyes
are protected now against the blaze

and the poem written beneath a cross
spiked on a Moorish rampart –
will it be picked up by happenstance
and help some loner face the glare?

C L Vinson

The Bench

The black cloud waltzes,
follows motor's whine,
burps power   pushes
caged bears down jammed city streets.

pedestrians cough
amidst
honking gazelles ushered
left   right
        between
green   red,

while curses fling insults
crammed against yellow lights.

In the middle on a paint chipped
bus bench
she sits
adorned in printed daisies
and buttercups framed in green
held, by this gray fortress.

Robots hustle
skinned in flesh,
pious eyes blind.

She stares into uncountable
vacant wishes
holding her tattered doll
whose one arm is twisted
and cracked,
the other lost in a garbage heap.

Skinny legs, dirty toes dangle.
Leather sandals bounce
above the silent rain.

Eleven summers witness
guilty this urchin's birth,
mingling pain
on reflective malleable cheeks.
She is mute-hearted
where rosebuds no longer grow.

Shadows in the night
in harsh reality
chase her to makeshift
huts, down alleys

and she dares to cry
only
beneath thunder
to hide her moans.

Memories of home fade
with broom handle beatings
void of compassion
echoed in alcohol stench
fuming from goodnight kisses
wax lips on tearful cheeks.

A wild *tsunami* scoops her up
into lifeless crowds
past the cold bench
leaves no trace of her existence.

Wedding Vows

5:17 pm
   soup boils
   underscoring the computer game
   her kids play,
husband home
   rush hour traffic
   banging rattle
   door slams,
grunts matrimony demands
   points to bedroom

she smells
   stale beer
   smoke stripper perfume
where he deposited school lunch money
   in a whore's G-string.

wife sits on mattress foot
   eyes cast down
   lifts skirt spreads
   hands folding twists gold band
aimlessly

she thinks of vacations never taken,

heavy breaths burp a few seconds
   he stuffs a wadded dollar
in her stretched panties,

soup burns.

Sister Clara's Prayer

she inhales the guarded fragrance
that dances in the hair of young boys
and steals away quietly to her
cloistered cell
and dreams of motherhood

standing nude
she imagines her full fruited womb
exploding with life,

and for the
sake of self-denial surrenders
to vows of habit
addicted to bare kneed prayers
she recites daily penance for
her sins
        but crosses heavenly gates
and asks

for a brief moment's slice
of eternity
        nine months of happiness
        to conceive and give birth

each morning she awakes
to rhythmic sandal scrapings
barren angelic visitations.

The Forgetting

It is the willingness to succumb
to a blank page
ink pours from our veins.
We watch the old woman holding a yellowed quill.

We, her successors, balance
on worn flat rockers
the grind of hickory on hickory
transforms us.

We wear her face
our eyes the colour of grass,
She sits, knits
smokes a cob-pipe.

An inner hunger tugs on us
like blunt horseshoe nails
draws deer hides tight.

She rocks forward
we rock, she purls, puffs
hums 'Amazing Grace'
thinks of slave days, revivals – freedom
and a stolen kiss against a camp meeting tent.
It's sweet, trembling
and the first.

The river sings
over red maples through willows
massages whispering pines.

Her dappled hands wash us
like ripples over river stones.

The Vendor of Love

The roadside is graced
    by her sitting
    on the corner
Demonstrating the sweetness of her
    grapes   cherries   and plums
Overflowing from wash-pails and baskets.
Fuzzy peaches
    prop lazily on her lap
caught in the folds of a
    harvest-green dress.
Figs laden with energy
    call out to me,
desiring as I desire.

Surrounded in this eden of fruit
I savour
    her passionate form the most.
Voluptuous breasts make cantaloups skrink.

        Thighs open
    streaming down from Bartlett Pear hips
creating the bottom of an hourglass
        holding pure sand.

She gives me ballast,
    a foundation
        with which to build.

She beckons me,
    not as a skinny signpost
but with open arms
    full and welcoming.

Reviews

The Timely Weed

The Bare Abundance, Selected Poems, 1975 – 2001, GF Dutton, Bloodaxe, £8.95

G F Dutton has released a book of poems every decade since the 70s. All have received awards and critical acclaim. However Dutton's poetry has been overshadowed by the scope and scale of his other activities and writings. Hard science, mountaineering, wild swimming, forestry and his cult success as a 'marginal gardener' have left his poetry almost taken for granted. Now the publication of his selected poems makes it impossible to dove-cote him as the Marvell-cum-Capability Brown of hyperborean terrain.

The selection is thematic not chronological. The four sections – 'City', 'Sea', 'Forest' and 'Rock' – represent life in society, physical and biological force and spiritual possibilities. None of these facets is experienced in isolation – there is a 'free exchange' of poems across the divisions from time to time. But the broad classification eases entry into Dutton's personal landscape. The composure of poems like 'The Concrete Garden' unifies the book.

> It takes time
> to become set. Before that
>
> you spread it out
> smack it, thrust
>
> bright-eyed advances
> about the agglomerate, sow
>
> whatever is new,
> is bound to grow,
>
> push through
> rise to you there – you
>
> regarding from heaven
> before the streets stiffen.
>
> Even then, they swear, one mushroom
> can break up a pavement.

The cerebral in Dutton is conveyed with a feather lightness. He is no stranger to irony or word play. Though both are understated.

> This is a street
> paved and flat, saying
> it leads somewhere.
> I shall take it

> but not seriously.
> It will lose itself
> in courts, piazzas
> a haggle
> of other streets, will end
> in some smoking crater.
> I shall take it
> as if at my pleasure ... 'Street'

He uses words sparingly ("Excess baggage hinders any journey"). His is a body of work without any needless fat. The verse is easy on the eye and ear. Delicate schemes of rhyme and assonance are almost invisible. Musicality is less difficult to miss. Read aloud, the verses sing as in 'The High Flats at Craigston'.

> the high flats at Craigston stand
> rawboned in a raw land,
> washed by thunderstorms and sun
> and cloud shadows rolling on
> from the bare hills behind, each one
> out-staring the wind;
> that every night
> cling together and tremble with light.

New readers to Dutton's work would benefit from starting with 'How Calm the Water'. This superb sequence on wild swimming is the acting out of a metaphor until there is no air left ("That was belief./ Being achieved/ for the price of a breath"). An identity rather than a likeness has been experienced. In one 12-cylinder intake the scope and exactitude of his poetry is caught.

The good gardener has to be organised or the weeds will take over. Dutton leaves enough to chance to surprise himself with an unexpected flower, a predatory deer or an archeological discovery, as in 'Roots':

> When we took up the roots we found
> they were long, perfectly sound
> and the better to grip had curled
> and split a great stone underground.

He allows a crack for the weed to appear:

> At the least the need
> to look about, decide
> what wild flower
> that once had lead you there
> is now a weed.('Culture')

The good scientist starts with a clear idea

which is tested against experience. Dutton proposes simple concepts whose exactness is questioned in the poem's development. In contrast to a fellow scientist-poet Miroslav Holub (who exploits ideas to show their inherent absurdity) Dutton fragments them into flints which spark off speculation and re-definition. It is as though he is returning ideas to the wild, observing their capacity to survive and transforming them through imaginative intervention when rescue is necessary.

The prologue poem, 'The Miraculous Issue', exemplifies this method. A spring that supplies his garden and house with water feels warm to the hand in winter and cold in the summer. But his thermometer finds it has a constant temperature of four degrees Celsius. Reality (the mind) and perception (the body) are at variance. But the power of the imagination, the instrument of poetry, is able to reconcile the apparent contradiction with the facts, the instrument of science ('for the water about my hand/ answers to life').

The 'City' section ends with three subtly unsettling poems. 'Occasion' encapsulates the sweet nervousness of a fifties wedding. 'New House in the Country' treats with a young married couple entering their first home and 'Stone' is about the rock that was too tough to shift and remained a silent presence on the threshold throughout a long marriage. "I remember it yellow, unblemished,/ a growing refusal in the sunlight/ and us kneeling before it/ sweating, dismantling its earth."

In Dutton's horticultural poems time is on the side of the poet. Winter may seem like death but it does not last foreve as in 'Faith.

I need no lifetime to enjoy
the flower that drinks its day of sky

or years of frost and hurricane
to praise the seed and plant again

for calendars no more apply
now I grow old and make my way

out of less likely spring after spring
into whatever is certain to be

far from this winter-blossoming
downside of eternity.

The last section, 'Rock', is a late flowering

of hard won delights: composing a pibroch in a volcano (extinct), breaking a glass at table and being too entranced by one's companion to notice, thus destroying a facile metaphor. Dutton, it seems to me, is defying a teasing complaint by a friendly reader ("My verse is not sufficiently explicit,/ does not reflect/ the human situation") with writing that flows so freely that you don't notice at first the spillage and human refraction that is the inevitable backdrop to life. The subject is the osmosis of self across borders and membranes and the paradoxical comfort of hard edges.

Here Dutton's love affair with Scotland flourishes beyond the generic versions in earlier sections. Place names appear like Proustian memories ("Butt of Lewis, Barra Head/ Barvas") and history locates a more peopled landscape in double time, now and before. Love/ hate perhaps allows the inclusion in this section of more conventional poems ('Goal', 'Visitation', 'Time'), relaxations in a stringently composed book. A more rigorous inclusion is his tribute to George Forrest, the great plant hunter, a *tour de force* of horticultural hyperbole which is wonderfully appropriate to the man and his *métier*.

Dutton in 'Barra' ('City') quotes Albert Speer's eerie epigram "one must build carefully/ to ruin well". He is not commenting on his own poetry, but on the fatalism of a world not given to seeking lasting solutions. Like Charles Rennie Mackintosh, in his late watercolours of Port-Vendres and the Pyrenean villages, Dutton has deployed his mastery of science to build poetry that houses his ideas and experience. I have Mackintosh's masterpiece 'The Rock' in mind. The foundations are sparely fissured rocks, riven if only to reformulate again in the artist's hands. Renewal is inbuilt. It is work that will weather well, as 'Drought' testifies:

Soil is dry.
roots meet rocks;
stem, bare sky.
Day after day
God's blue eye
measures the earth again …

Augustus Young

The Edinburgh International Book Festival 2003

Never judge a Book Festival by its sponsor's supplement cover. Having learnt the hard way with a record number of cancellations in 2002, *The Herald/ Sunday Herald* waited mere weeks before the event in August to publish its highlights of the Festival ahead. Then they featured on their cover Candace Bushnell, "iconic creator" of *Sex and the City* (a TV "bratshow" I'm told). Alan Taylor, meeting her in New York, reported she had a "cutely pointed" chin. This surely was a Festival that brought to Edinburgh Mario Vargas Llosa, Alastair Reid, Susan Sontag, Jennifer Johnston, John Irving and Doris Lessing.

It was also a Festival with the most stimulating poetry programme in years, due to a series of individual performances rather than 'big' names. This should not diminish its overall effect – a triumph for Catherine Lockerbie in her third year as director. She was a little perturbed by my column in *Chapman* 102-3 about last year's Festival, but, as she told me and Miranda Rankin at the opening performance (a poetry reading), she found the experience "cathartic". We beamed at each other for the next fortnight.

She is above criticism, as became clear in her counter-attack on Christopher Harvie, who found this year's programme "Big Apple writ large global", and the Festival itself an "institute" not serving Scotland well (*The Scotsman*, 17 June). She put him in his place: "There are more than 100 Scottish writers in the adult programme", she replied (18 June) – out of 550 authors attending. Support came from Lorraine Fannin (Scottish Publishers Association) who took umbrage at Harvie's reference to a "raging mob from Jenner's tearoom". Alan Taylor told us it did not matter that Harvie's "cage was rattled". He lives in Germany so what could he know about matters in Charlotte Square?

I clearly recall that long ago another academic, Prof N Craig Sharp, asserted that "Edinburgh has three Graces of literature in

Joy Hendry of *Chapman*, Tessa Ransford of *Lines Review* and … Catherine Lockerbie" (Letter in *The Scotsman*, 9 February 1996). What Lockerbie has done is to enlarge the number of events and authors attending, and so claim "record" attendances and sales. But does this sacrifice quality, I asked last year. "Why the negativity?" she replied. So here I go, reproved but not reformed.

Over the last two decades poetry has been well-represented in sessions in the Spiegeltent. There have also been moments of individual wonder – especially Charles Causley (1987), Yehuda Amichai (1995), Lucien Stryk (1998) and the unforgetable "rendering" into English by Seamus Heaney last year of Sorley MacLean's 'Hallaig'. This year a palpable sense of absence hovered in the mind. Visitors and locals raised standards in unconscious tribute to Edwin Morgan.

Brian Taylor echoed that when introducing Poet Laureate Andrew Motion at the first "Wake up to Words" session. Morgan was to have shared the platform with Motion. The Englishman read, in an understated fashion, most movingly, two of Morgan's poems from his recent collection *Love and Life* (Mariscat £9.00). From his own work he initially read amusing and anecdotal poems, "snaps", and then read with elegance and integrity (and for the first time in Scotland) the long poem 'Serenade', the name of the horse that threw his mother. For ten years until her death she was in a coma. He was sixteen at the time of the accident. With unsentimental depth and revealing power the poetry programme had begun.

Another near-capacity audience held their breath as coughing fits racked John Burnside and Don Patterson. The poems, however, emerged, timely and focused. Burnside's new work is infused by a spiritual dimension that has secular clarity. Patterson is a puzzle. I recall an arrogant performance in East Anglia which alienated the audience. His performance in Edinburgh was slow burning and sublime. Maybe fatherhood (twin sons) has mellowed him – and definitely inspired him.

Reading from his new collection *Landing Light* he entered the mind as a friend. At peace with his creativity he writes "the dark is my sounding board, the light / my auditorium".

Another meeting and yet a contrast of minds marked the session with Gillian Ferguson and Stewart Conn. She, an "on-going" mother, read wonderfully tender poems from her collection *Baby*. He mined memories of stone inscriptions to evoke love and in the illuminating 'Renoir in Orkney' recreates an artist who "will distribute at the solstice / canvases of wild flowers, like mottled flame."

The first week closed with an inspired grouping. Douglas Dunn ("for the first time I'm the youngest on the platform"), Anthony Thwaite and the sharp-witted Welshman Dannie Abse. Dunn was succinct and droll. Abse's poems never fail to impress with their humane championing of the underdog. Any and all underdogs: the would-be suicide on the Irish ferry; the savaged black in an American bus station; even the bigot in his surgery (Abse is a GP). The most powerful poem tells of a racially abusive patient who is maybe unaware that Abse is both Celt and Jew. The medic is tempted to retribution. The poet instead concentrates on life's contradictions. Thwaite's technically concise poems work better on the page yet I was intrigued to learn that he taught one Cadet Gaddaffi "English for Special Purposes" when tutor for the British Council in Libya during the '60s.

For unexplained reasons the prestigious Griffin Poetry Prize for Excellence in Poetry ($40,000) was tucked away mid-day in the small Field and Lawn Marquee. Another disappointment was the absence of Kathleen Jamie. The Canadian Award went to the severe Margaret Avison. The International Award deservedly went to Irishman Paul Muldoon for *Moy Sand and Gravel*. Graciously accepting the cheque he followed with a reading of majestic resonance. Unfortunately he was interrupted by loud liquid-fuelled alarms and clamours from nearby. He paused to remark "it always sounds much more interesting out there". As I discovered later, the noise came from a book launch in an adjacent tent. Sadly this collision of events also meant many Scottish poets and writers at the launch failed to hear a poet of international renown at his peerless best.

An afternoon session with Roddy Lumsden and Kate Clanchey again allowed differences in approach. Her poems of pregnancy and later on "release" into parenthood contrasted in an almost surreal way with the empirical earthiness of Lumsden's detailed observations. There was almost a spat. She fulminated at the fee paid for inclusion in a school anthology (£17.50). He whispered that "she would be on everybody's lips". She pouted. He blushed. Next morning saw two warriors of peace speak of elements of war. Alan Spence "interpreting loosely, very loosely" from the Japanese of Ryokan (1758-1831) read "Its pissin dooon / ah'm drookit – / this is it." Christopher Logue, drawing from Homer, gave us a mesmerising rhythmic reading from *War Music*. Here the parallel texts of conceit lead to abandoned brutalities and compassion – drawing the warmth of love even from designated enemies.

Any and all of these performances would have ensured this to be a memorable festival. But the final days brought more and more of the same. Robert Crawford opened with a pulsating "version" of the 1411 "evocation to war" for the Clan Donald before going into battle at Harlew. "Be eager, be excellent, be eagles, be elegant." In his following poems elegance became versified, his love poems became "declarations of dependence". His fellow reader was W N Herbert who moved from reportage to mayhem with skill and confidence, reading from his *Big Bumper Book of Troy*. He concluded with an epitaph for a friend that became a celebration of a life.

Celebration is the middle name of Alastair Reid. It is a great joy that he is now a regular visitor and reader at the Festival. I first heard him in 1987 when he read twice and since then he has become a Must See, Hear and Learn from the presence of this writer.

On the final day came Robin Robertson and

Carol Ann Duffy. It was a pleasure to hear Robertson's graceful and erudite ode to Edinburgh's Camera Obscura. However it was the preparation and delivery of Duffy's half-hour that rounded off the entire seventeen days for me. Reading alternately from *The World's Wife* and *Feminine Gospels*, she gave us an object lesson in how to entrap and then enthrall an audience by making the telling of stories into a poetic tale. Wonderful.

If the poetry was elevating, the prose was often dull. Mostly when it involved journalists who were designated 'commentators'. More than 70 appeared this year, some more than once. Years ago Norman Mailer spoke of the relationship between authors and audiences in Charlotte Square as akin to "Christian missionaries confronting cannibals". Many press-related events were packed by fellow hacks hovering like misplaced vampires before the lights went up; self-preening led to chat-show orations. The worst offenders were Peter Hitchins and William Deedes followed by a writer I admire, Roy Greenslade. Opinions were delivered as judgements. Often it was great fun but in the end words entered prepared phrases and emerged as new-minted clichés empty of import.

There was the odd exception, as when Doris Lessing and Christopher Hope talked of common and contemporary problems in their homeland in southern Africa. Apartheid, Mugabe and media reporting were talked about in uncomfortable proximity. Chair Magnus Linklater, columnist and former editor of *The Scotsman*, became censorious. Hope bristled and Lessing bridled. Hope turned the conversation. He talked eloquently of "British press complicity with government policy" not only during the Falklands War but also during the current Gulf conflict. "An attitude more than reminiscent of the bad years in South Africa", concluded Hope. Doris cackled. Questions from the floor were predictable. Liberal in tone, replied to with more of same. Then in the final minutes a hand which had been studiously ignored rose. "As a black African I strongly resent and object to you three presuming to compare the Apartheid regime with current events in Zimbabwe." That was as far as he got. The platform stood firm and revived their selective condemnation.

This was initially more informatively alarming than Ben Okri, who also questioned the motivation behind self-censorship in his short but important Scottish PEN Lecture. We swallow what we hear in the media, misinformation as well as information, he implied. He asked that conscience once again be allowed to control our responses to the events surrounding us. There was nothing new or controversial here, but I found it bleak that press coverage complained about the brevity of his speech rather than consider its content. Is the consumer the new controller?

There was an echo of this dilemma in Ariel Dorfman's Amnesty International Lecture later that week. Dorfman, exiled by Pinochet from Chile, has not always persuaded me as a playwright or fiction writer, but here he was a credible polemicist. Like Susan Sontag he used the photographic image as the immediate conduit to the mind. He admitted to being "incurably, tragically optimistic". He raged against indifference. As Rosemary Goring in her splendid piece in *The Herald* wrote, "Nobody forces you to forget. His conclusion was a call to collective responsibility. It was a stirring ending to a memorable hour that bore testimony to the power of putting aside self-pity and choosing instead to make the world a better place for others." Goring as *The Herald*'s literary editor has shown admirable confidence in pricking the vanities (Sontag) and praising the brash entertainment value of others (Irving and Bushnell). I regret *The Herald*'s use of star evaluation for individual events, but fortunately Goring's words justified her evaluations. (*****).

Scottish Gaelic was given a singular airing to mark two books of prose fiction. Having listened to the stories of Martin MacIntyre, and moving excerpts from Angus Peter Campbell's first novel, I, dictionary aflutter, look forward to reading both in my own time.

Way back in the first week there was literally a dramatic reconstruction of a flyting, as Owen Dudley Edwards and Oscar Wilde's grandson Merlin Holland played out the real trial of Wilde, which was his confrontation with fellow Dubliner Edward Carson in court. Owen doing a north Dublin accent as Carson was worth the bellyache from laughter.

There were moments of grief, none more than the confrontation between Palestinian Raja Shehadeh and Bernard Wasserstein – August 20th, the day after bombing and retaliation in Baghdad and Jerusalem claimed over 30 lives. As these men found ideology useless to enclose their anger, I regret to say Chair Chris Doal was out of his depth. Too nice a man. The invocation of an Irish background as a means of understanding the tension each side of him was sadly misplaced.

Another Failure in the Chair was Simon Fanshawe, having prepared for a cosy fellow-gay chat with novelist Edmund White, who was speechless when the American chose to concentrate on the "new racism" he sees in post-September 11 2001 America. Incidentally, like Dorfman, White also refered to another 11/9; that of 1973 when the CIA colluded in the overthrow of the elected government in Chile. Maybe Fanshawe was tired. According to the funniest piece on the Festival, David Robinson in *The Scotsman*, he had been taken apart by Ms Bushnell in a dark tent the night before. The dear boy should not have questioned her "niceness". Four letter words can be implosive.

I should not question the enjoyment I have had this year. But good humour should not distract from bad habits. Catherine Lockerbie's programming is still a mess. For too many days choice is still dictated by exclusion rather than inclusion. Yet I was not worried by ticket limitations as in 2002. Particular thanks to Olivier Joly and Louise Anderson in the Press Office (I refuse to call it a Pod). I regret to see Ms Anderson has been co-opted by Scottish Book Trust. The post of Marketing and PR Manager for EIBF is up for grabs again (£25,000-£26,000). A third such change in as many years.

So a final roll call – fiction writers who are not journalists, which exempts one South American whose self-promotion this year was as unchanged as his hair style. Do or dye. The encounter between Allan Massie and Nicholas Mosley was hi-jacked by Chair Magnus Linklater's obsessive interest in his stepmother who had died the day before (Mosley's stepmother Diana). As Doris Lessing said "we honour the dead and all too often fail to respect the wounded and the living".

There was a gloriously subversive morning with Ali Smith and Lucy Ellmann. The detailed account of Edinburgh's sewers caused croissant to be spluttered and coffee to grow cold. Ellman's partner Todd McEwan reading from his new novel showed a similar interest in the broadening of the bowel. The other two novelists that captured the mind and sent me back to their books were Jennifer Johnston reading from *This Is Not A Novel* and Colum McCann taking us behind the stage for a life of Nureyev. Movement caught in spare but evocative prose in *Dancer*. And then there were encounters with Ian Rankin. I departed his interview with Paul Johnston ever more convinced that in Rankin we have an investigative Stevenson. His "precipitious city" reveals heights that conceal depths.

Favourite moments: Benign Richard Holloway allowing First Minister McConnell to read from Roald Dahl's *Big Friendly Giant*, watched by Kirsty Wark, without even a reference to a large monument to the mercenaries at the foot of Holyrood. Fintan O'Toole, unwittingly echoing the freestyle ad-lib love of Shakespeare that made Tariq Ali such fun on the opening day. The freefalling compassion embraced by Holloway in his unscripted appeal for tolerance in the concluding event. He was talking of morals and ethics.

Final word from poet Don Patterson speaking of the performer as "fifth in the company of four". Compound the numbers and I will distill the pleasure of this year. Thank you, *Chapman*, for letting me record my thoughts.

Hayden Murphy

Theatre Roundup 2003 Festival

Have We Got What It Takes?

In September, just after the 2003 Edinburgh Festival, the National Theatre of Scotland (NToS) became a real commitment. Have we got what it takes to do Scotland proud, theatrically? The only Scottish production on the stages of the EIF was the premiere of David Greig's *San Diego*, by Glasgow Tron Theatre. This best-known and prolific Scottish playwright co-directed with Marisa Zanotti.

After his acclaimed *Outlying Islands* in the 2002 Traverse Festival programme, this had Greig back to his more fascinating and accomplished style where stories mix and separate. Set in San Diego, Britain and in a jet plane, the play explores our modern "always on the move" world where children in affluent nations spend more time in aeroplanes than with their grandparents. The pilot of Greig's plane is the central character. His son Andrew is an actor, playing a pilot in a film in California, while his disturbed daughter in London, Laura, has a hunger she fills by eating, shockingly, herself. In her hospital there is a patient, David, with whom she forms a strange and essential bond as love emerges as the painful, imperilled and moving centre of many of the play's relationships.

Greig's play demands an engaged audience. There are twelve characters to follow in multiple scenes which are switched between in a directorial version of channel hopping. The effort is rewarded by a play containing openness, lightening humour along with a theatrical capturing of our world's challenges, where it's possible to travel all over but never find a home.

Simon Vincenzi's set, with many suitcases and items of our anonymous modern lives, gave the Lyceum stage the illusion of spacious width. In a procession of short scenes, the play disquietingly draws in the threads. The stories reveal that the ones closest and most in touch with themselves live in the frailest ways. Many of us have learnt to treat our lives as the Pilot does his occupation, "it's a practical job, you get on with it and don't dwell". The sadness, and anguish of that reality suffuses Greig's play in the characters' delicately hinged lives and in a funeral with only two mourning friends.

Over on the Fringe a number of plays came from Scottish companies in as great variety as it is intended our national theatre will commission. We saw not only companies used to appearing in Scotland's prestige theatres, but also work and companies going into the smallest of venues, and even outside. One of the biggest hits of the Fringe was Grid Iron's *Those Eyes, That Mouth*, directed by Ben Harrison. This production took place in a building part way through renovation. The audience gazed up and down staircases, grouped in rooms inside a play full of images.

The most arresting one revealed a stream and the scent of growing released by the removal of a dustsheet. Cait Davis's Woman was retreating from the world, caught in that more than half-mad state when relationships go west and betrayal and shame make you lose your centre. Singer David Paul Jones's presence was also often the unspeaking ex-lover, his male presence adding piquancy of lost desire and future. Grid Iron display again how they fuse strong story, heightened intensity, images, place and acting, giving to their audience the powerful role of witness.

Theatre Babel brought Liz Lochhead's *The Thebans*, based on the classical plays about the Kingdom of Thebes, directed by Graham McLaren. It brought together stories, dramatised by Sophocles, Euripides and Aeschylus, of the fated family of Oedipus, stories which today are often unknown apart from Freudian reference. Jennifer Black was a memorable Jokasta; a woman who finds her second marriage to Oedipus is a ghastly mismatch. Nowadays with such a marriage between parent and child more likely and our sense of abomination diminished, some of the play's force is reduced. Other themes of what is honourable, traitorous and how people are swept unconsulted in a ruler's wake come through.

But the production was flawed by the

136

weight of events to cover in a two-hour performance. The most dislocating example was
the casting of Tireias with a female actor,
played in unexplained bare-breastedness.
Only those who knew Greek mythology
(Tireias was turned into a woman by the Gods
as punishment for killing a female snake)
could add the essential understanding. Most of
the audience were confused, embarrassed or
enraged that a female actor was stumbling
about the stage, her top half exposed due, as
they saw it, to a director's wilful whim.

England's Paines Plough brought to the
Traverse Gregory Burke's *The Straits*,
directed by John Tiffany. He also directed
Burke's successful *Gagarin Way* which the
Traverse premiered at the 2001 Fringe. Set on
Gibraltar as the Falklands Task Force goes
south, *The Straits* has three boys and a girl, all
under 18. Their retreat is a concrete bathing
spot, on The Rock, because their families
work for the British military. Burke's characters are confronted by their limited and chill-
ing world view, one shared by many fellow
Brits. Tiffany's direction ensured the young
cast developed with the well-structured text in
an often painful reminder of how we abandon
youth and youths too often. Neil Warming-
ton's set suggested not only the surrounding
depths of the sea but also the unseen dangers
of life in its simplicity.

Also at the Traverse Richard Wilson
directed Tales Told by An Idiot/ The Royal
Court's production of the Presnyakov Brothers' *Playing The Victim*. This Siberian text
was played in vaudeville style with pace and
intelligence. A commission involving Wilson, a director/ actor of considerable skill too
rarely seen on home ground, could be worth
considering for an early NToS production.

The Traverse Theatre itself staged two new
plays, Henry Adam's *The People Next Door*
and David Harrower's *Dark Earth*. Adam's
play like Burke's had one Scot, Mrs Mac,
Eileen McCallum, whose wee rants on *Take
The High Road* were particularly appreciated
by fans in the audience. Another gem is the
no-hoper Nigel played by Fraser Ayers. Nigel

is the kind of guy we pass by. After spending
the play in his company, his off-the-wall view
of the hell that is modern life for the underdog,
reminds that those at the bottom of the shit
heap can still be sterling characters.

Written quickly and submitted to the
Traverse on 1st April, Adam's play sparkles
with sharp observation and a believable variety of contemporary characters. When Nigel's
flat gains guests in neighbours Mrs Mac and
black schoolboy Marco, the weak together
find a strength. Adam gives the Scottish canon
that rare thing, a life-strengthening play with
a disquieting and highly subversive twist.
Could he be developing into a Dario Fo with
extra attitude?

A contrasting disappointment was David
Harrower's play *Dark Earth*, directed by
Philip Howard. It was difficult to find anything worth digging out of this ill-structured
play which had characters revealing things
suddenly rather than believably. Some new
plays spring up vibrant and unforgettable.
Dark Earth, despite a strong cast, was not
planted with any memorable moments.

Set by the Antonine Wall, an urban couple
find themselves stranded and then delayed by
the family they seek support from. Not only
did the play grow its fruits from unconsoli-
dated ground, the production too made unfor-
tunate choices, involving the overpowering
set with its huge stone wall and the farmhouse
conservatory. Until they were glass walled in
the final clunking scene, the latter's boundaries were blithely walked through by the cast.

Judy Steel's Rowan Tree Theatre Company
brought John Carnegie's drama based on
Hogg's *The Private Memoirs and Confession
of a Justified Sinner*. Directed by Carnegie,
this script goes deep into the Calvinist heart of
the Scottish soul. Matthew Burgess as The
Suicide and Alan Steele as Gil-Martin and
other characters were magnificently cast.

Sarah Colvin's *Meat* was premiered by Nut-
shell in The Underbelly, a venue we could do
with all year round. Containing fantasy
moments drawing on *film noir*, *Meat*'s comic
feel was like that of *Playing the Victim*. Kate

Nelson demanded ironic performances from her Scottish cast. They were delivered with relish. Criticised by some as over-cooked, others savoured its flavour.

At Roxy Art House, a venue now available outside the Festival, Laboratorium-33 performed in a space reminiscent of the Citizen's Stalls Studio. David Priestly's play, *Digging For Fire*, lacked coherence despite Laura Cameron Lewis and Simon Tcherniak's portrayals as the two couples (or was it one?). One struggles to live together, the other to survive a civil war. The Scottish National Theatre, with its commissioning rather than building-based form, has a healthy variety of Scottish theatre to draw on.

The NToS should enable shows designed for formal theatres to be performed in different venues, instead of the short three week or less excellent productions have had. It makes better theatrical, as well as economic, sense to give notable productions wider audiences. In addition the NToS model should include theatre on the hoof, in buildings or other spaces – forests, sports centres and disused factories, taking theatre into communities. There's an exhilaration released when a production is given to audiences so they experience it in part of their home environment.

Recent Edinburgh's August Festivals have more Scottish companies and playwrights premiering new work. In 2003 our showings suggest we *do* have the talent necessary to make our unique model of a National Theatre work. Now it is clear the notion of theatre has widened well beyond the conventional front-on-stage and numbered seating; we have shown some Scots cunning in avoiding the building-based trap. This year again proved that there's enough ability and creativity to make the NToS distinctive and energising.

Thelma Good

Published Texts

San Diego by David Greig, *Dark Earth* by David Harrower, *The Straits* by Gregory Burke, Faber 2003; *Thebans* by Liz Lochhead, *Playing The Victim* by Presnyakov Brothers and *The People Next Door* by Henry Adam, Nick Hern Books 2003.

Pamphleteer

Poetry still continues to dominate pamphleteer publishing in Scotland and the rest of Britain. The projects here mentioned make us believe that, in these cases, the content fits the medium perfectly. *Waiting for the End* (Lomond Press, 4 Whitecraigs, Kinesswood, Kinross, £5.00) covers poems from R L Cook's fifty years of writing. Although the verse has previously appeared elsewhere, this is a rare chance to contemplate the diversity of Cook's poetic approaches to existence. He lets his language take over the verse and the stanza, whether influenced by concrete experiences or incarnating some vague abstract voice. The pamphlet includes verse in Scots and translations of François Copée. A wise purchase.

Congratulations to Aggie Weston's Editions (37, Laund Close, Belper, Derbyshire) for four excellent poetry selections and their pleasant design (£4.50 each or all four at a reduced rate). These small numbers (eight poems each) of the *PoetsPoems* Series are the responsibility of Thomas A Clark, Gael Turnbull, Simon Cutts and Allan Halsey. They constitute an apparently personal choice of verse from the most diverse authors (Pound, Joyce, W C Williams, Browning, Appolinaire, among many others), and turn out to be a really unique opportunity to get acquainted with contemporary voices that you would be otherwise unlikely to encounter. It feels like being taken by the hand inside a very good poetry library. It's hard to say which is the best selection (Clark's is a personal favourite), although the nature of the work becomes clearer when taken as a whole. The pamphlets fit perfectly in any glove compartment – handy for a long traffic jam. We are reliably informed more poets have agreed to choose their favourite relics.

A special mention to Corbie Press (57 Murray St., Montrose, Angus, Scotland) and their Poets Series No 8 and 9 (£3.00). Despite the simple cover design, George Hardie's *In Transit* and Lilian Anderson's *Stanes and*

Leaves are two inspiring poetry books. Mostly in Scots, Hardie's *In Transit* gathers poems from a wide range of urges and themes. The verse is in most cases gentle and fluid, whether in dedicatory style (to Hugh MacDiarmid or John MacLean) or in a quiet recollection of past images. It certainly deserves a place on your bedside table. Also in Scots, Anderson struggles to overcome death and the shadow it casts upon the landscapes, the seasons and every moment of the day. It is a brave task, mostly accomplished by her constantly dealing with ghosts through language. The voice of the poems finds itself troubled by memory but seemingly assisted by the presence of other poets. Days are handled one by one between deep loss and a (perhaps false) quietness. The conclusion "no use crying over spilt blood/ or cheap wine" might seem to be despair disguised in humorous irony. This is truly one to read.

The South African Stanley Trevor brings us *Black Edged Mountains Cut the Sky: A Scottish Journey* (Anarcho Press, 7 Portland Terrace, Nairn, £3.00). The pamphlet is a small acknowledgement of the poet's new home and consequently new identity. It is very rare to come across such a surprisingly heartfelt description of landscapes. Every element seems to have its own presence, its own living body. The conciseness and rhythm of some of the language employed sometimes resemble Native American oral literature, honest and solemn. Trevor is also rather adventurous in terms of form and the use of metaphor ('Landscapes' is a good example of both these abilities). An insightful visit to the heart of Scottish nature.

Ian Revie is another travelling poet. *The Walrus Tusk and the Dancing Bear* (Akros, 33 Lady Nairn Avenue, Kirkcaldy, Fife, £4.75) might sound like a children's book, but is actually a poetic incursion into the possibilities of a compromise between home and the urge of 'otherness'. But this does not say much about the poems themselves. That is mainly because the readers will be facing a fierce and explosive language, travelling as fast as thought itself ('Lingua Franca', for instance, illustrates that search for suitable language, for an appropriate verse). Occasionally, the page is overpopulated with both meaningful and expendable references. Nevertheless, a nice option for a lazy afternoon.

Oher pamphlets from Akros (£2.75) to be mentioned: *Tales from a Small Island* is Cheryl Follon's first poetry collection, mostly structured in single-stanza episodes propelled by a rhyming motion that might not attract everyone. Follon is a storyteller, hence the kind of narrative nature of the whole pamphlet. These verses' secret voice does not reveal much of itself, although the opening poem 'Certainties' seemingly allows some level of intimacy with the reader. Some might not be impressed by Follon's intense desire of "telling stories and poems and dancing", but there are nevertheless tales of true lives in these compositions. Alexander Hutchinson's *Sparks in the Dark* is a feast for the senses in its daring mixture of subtle grace and (almost) tragic irony. He trusts his poems enough not to lengthen them unnecessarily, so that at the end of each there is always that pleasant aura of indeterminacy. Hutchinson shows how humorous poetry can be, and how incredibly surprising. These are shining sparks.

A brief word about the 2001 and 2002 Poetry Workshops of the Society of Civil and Public Service Writers. Its participants have been gathered in two interesting poetry pamphlets, which might convince other civil servants to take part in future. Both entitled *Waves* (Bill Douglas, 47 Walkerston Avenue, Largs, Ayrshire, £2.00 each), the collections are not quite consistent in style, quality or inspiration (which hardly could be expected from such an anthology). Although one or two poems are not enough to get acquainted with an author, this will hopefully motivate others to organise similar workshops. A poem printed is a poem saved.

As usual, translation also marks its presence in pamphlet publication. In *The Poems of Sulpicia* (Hearing Eye, 99 Torriano Avenue, London), John Heath-Stubbs gives us the opportunity to discover "the only woman poet of ancient Rome whose name and work have come down to us". It is a small book, in proportion to our knowledge of Sulpicia's life and personality. But the poems truly bear the honesty of language and the passionate feeling that certainly still appeals to the reader almost two thousand years after. It might even arouse an interest in discovering other classical poets. Certainly worth a look.

A lot has already been written and debated regarding the events of September 2001 and the resulting 'war on terror'. Pierre Watter's *September 11th 2001: A New World* (Anarcho Press, £3.50) is a frightening yet admirable sum-up of the reasons why one should be suspicious of the US's conduct in the affair. It truly shows how disturbing it can be once one starts to unveil the whole plot. Watter is convincing and provides a diversity of solid bases for his arguments. By placing both the September 11 attacks and America's subsequent wars within a foreign policy strategy dating back to the cold war, Watters manages to put the issue in perspective, offering the reader a wider, more significant picture. This is a clear and honest book, which demands to be read.

Finally, drama also appears in this constellation by way of Louise Byres' *Painkillers* (New Century, 9 Trotsworth Court, Virginia Waters, £4.99). This three-act play takes place in a hospital ward where seven women gradually reveal themselves to each other. The text was apparently the happy result of the playwright's own experience in a public hospital, after having broken a leg. For the author's own sake, we hope she didn't have to spend much time with a person such as Lynn. The characters (Lynn being the ruling talkative one) evolve from superficial dialogue to a deep sense of communion, which the presence of illness certainly helps. *Painkillers* is a fine illustration of that (supposedly) feminine feeling of affiliation. Perhaps new and innovative theatre groups should explore material such as this.

João Henriques

Catalogue 104

Starting with the death of a blaspheming law student and ending with the robbery/ liberation of the Stone of Scone, Arthur Herman's *The Scottish Enlightenment* (4th Estate, £20.00) is a wide-ranging survey of Scottish thought and action from the 17th to the 20th century. While he ploughs the orthodox furrow, Herman also creates an illuminating, eventful history that is always engaging.

Alasdair Gray: Critical Appreciations and a Biography (British Library, £20.00), is a smorgasbord of adulation for Glasgow's renaissance man. With its arresting cover of Gray's greatest hits, writer after writer piles on the praise – from Kevin Williamson's coming of age with *Lanark* to Angus Calder's ruminations on Gray's (inter)nationalism, you are bowled over by the warmth of the tributes. Most are well done, but you can't help feeling that adoration has tossed critical thought out of the window somewhat. But a truly indispensable work – a collection of the man's art – has yet to appear.

Paul Henderson Scott speaks fondly of Gray's *A Twentieth-Century Life* (Argyll, £20.00), and Gray must think likewise, doing an almost regal profile sketch of Scott for the cover. Scott writes engagingly on his days in the Diplomatic Service. His 'return home' to Edinburgh is equally lively, with his career as cultural activist, SNP member and presence at any arts event of consequence.

Another hive of activity was Hugh Miller, celebrated in a reprint of his autobiography, *My Schools and Schoolmasters* (Black & White, £9.99). Born 1802, Miller rose from austere beginnings to become a writer, journalist and world-class authority on geology. Although the text is unsympathetically laid-out (eyes may water after a few pages) – the content is always involving. Time to appreciate one of Scotland's forgotten sons.

Another neglected native talent, John Macmurray, is the subject of a new biography, (Floris Books, £20.00). John E Costello has done his homework on the philosopher, delving into unpublished diaries and other sources with zeal. He tackles the theory well, although is less convincing on Macmurray's day-to-day matters. Nonetheless, this is a fitting tribute to a subtle and brilliant thinker.

Scottish Writers Talking 2 (Tuckwell, £9.99) is that rare beast, a collection of sustained interviews with writers. Isobel Murray (editor and main interviewer) has picked five inimitable authors – any one worth the price alone. Although the Iain Banks' interview was in 1988, it is none the worse for that – he talks about his background, his reading of *Reader's Digest* aged seven, career as a Costings Clerk and much else, all with good humour. The piece on Iain Crichton Smith is more an informal chat between old friends than an interview. Space precludes discussion of others – Bernard McLaverty, Naomi Mitchison and Alan Spence – but Murray pulls something special out of all. Buy it!

From one difficult task to an impossible one – George Barker's biography *The Chameleon Poet* by Robert Fraser (Cape, £25.00). Barker declared the task of his biography impossible, even to the lengths of mixing up journal records and misdating documents to fox anyone was foolish enough to try. But Fraser has assembled the life of one of the great men of 20th century English poetry into order. An enigma to his family, a source of worship to T S Eliot and an enviable lady's man to Dylan Thomas, Barker was an artistic dynamo whose talent required more praise than he got. Fraser is to be congratulated on this piece of detective work.

In Fraser's work, Barker recalls warmly Edwin Muir's early guidance and mentorship. But Hugh MacDiarmid had an altogether more explosive relationship with Muir – dwelt upon in length in MacDiarmid's *New Selected Letters* (Carcanet, £39.95). The venom in the spat over the use of Lallans as a viable langue can still be felt in a letter to Muir's son, Gavin in 1975: "I think time has proved me right and your father wrong". Apart from such fireworks, this book is an eye-opener on the sheer amount and variety of letters he wrote – to his friends Norman Mac-Caig, Sorley MacLean and others. Whether writing on pub opening hours or more serious topics, MacDiarmid always leaves a definite impression of his opinions.

Another giant of Scottish literature, Iain Crichton Smith, is celebrated in style in two volumes of his short stories: *The Red Door* (1949-76) and *The Black Halo* (1977-98) (Birlinn, both £9.99). While Smith has received much praise for his poetry, his short stories are less well known and are here in force. Editor Kevin McNeil, fighting his way through the mass of manuscripts left, provides an illuminating introduction to stories which givie a tantalising insight into one of Scotland's great writers. To truly do justice to his reputation though, Birlinn might consider publishing Smith's Gaelic stories. McNeil would make an excellent editor.

Is Robin Jenkins, according to his press release, 'Scotland's greatest living novelist?' Messrs Gray and Banks might also have a claim on that title, but Jenkins' *Poor Angus* and *Childish Things* (Canongate, £6.99 and £9.99) are not to be missed all the same. Whether it's high jinks on the Western Isles between an artist and his beautiful muse in *Poor Angus*, or a retired schoolmaster's eye for the ladies in *Childish Things*, Jenkins' writing flows like water, refreshing in its apparent simplicity. For a writer nearly in his 80s and with a vast back catalogue, the quality on display here is spellbinding.

Crashing onto the desk from Germany is *Babel* issue 12 (£9.00) – a special Scottish issue, no less. Iain Crichton Smith, George Mackay Brown and Edwin Morgan are some of the big hitters who feature while Robin Fulton is a very mischievous, but informative interviewee. Never stuck for a word or six, he lets rip on poetry readings; on reworking poems at proof stage: 'CERTAINLY NOT!' and translations, to amongst other subjects. His interview, along with unpublished work by Edwin Morgan *et al*, make this a worthwhile volume, although for only 80 pages, it's rather pricey. The absence of Scottish women doesn't help.

Another volume from the Babel stable is a bilingual selection of George Mackay Brown entitled: *Staubkorn Vom Boden Des Himmels* ('Grain Of Dust From The Floor of Heaven'. Babel is to be congratulated on further extending the international profile of Mackay Brown to German-speaking students of Scottish literature. One point of note is a diverting afterword by the translator on Brown's life and influences. (Babel Verlag, Kevin Perryman, Lorrenz-Paul-Strasse 4, Postfach 1, 86920 Denklingen, Germany).

Two new literary magazines demanding attention arrive. *Anon* (£4.00) is a brave new venture – choosing poems on their content, with authors only known on publication. Editor Mike Stocks makes a thoughtful, well-argued case for anonymity in his editorial, and also the counter-arguments – for future discussion – and the poetry is good too. *Sand* (£5.00) from north-east England takes almost a diametrically opposite approach – showing us the poet's biographies before we've read a word. While the poetry is good, the layout is occasionally distracting – too many fonts too big, text not justified – weakening an otherwise diverting collection. But for a first issue it's impressive and well-presented. Both *Anon* and *Sand* deserve watching.

'Soor Plums in Galashiels' and 'Willie Brew'd a Peck o' Maut' are just two of the more arresting song titles in J Murray Neil's *The Scots Fiddle: Volume 2* (Neil Wilson Publishing, £20.00), which concentrates on the Lothians, Ayrshire and the Borders. This revised, expanded version of the previous volume gives notation to the songs and background notes on the history of the area and the composer. While the notation will be for fiddlers only, the notes and atmospheric illustrations will enlighten us to the key role they played in Scottish history and culture.

Fragments of Union: Making Connections in Scottish and American Writing by Susan Manning (Palgrave, £42.50) concentrates on an ill-considered subject. Manning makes interesting assertions, notably that the writings of the Scottish Enlightenment helped fuel the American Revolution. Also, that debates over association between Scotland and England had their mirror across the Atlantic. However, the writing is often too dry, thick with references and academese. The reader will have to use a linguistic machete to hack through the undergrowth.

An entirely different effort is Carla Sassi's *Imagined Scotlands* (Edizioni Parnaso, 14.20 Euro/ $14.00) which takes a provacative look at Scottish literature from the Renaissance to the present through the lens of post-colonial analysis. Sassi teases apart the creation of a British culture and the attempted displacement of Scottish culture, the interplay of identity and difference within such a field and the limits of her approach. There are individual chapters on works by James MacPherson, Walter Scott, Lorna Moon and a biography of Robert Burns by Catherine Carswell. Readers enticed by the above should note that the book is in Italian. Sassi is to be congratulated on her adventurous spirit – sailing into relatively unknown waters in Italian academia.

Like academia, economics is an area where you would expect to be confronted with impenetrable jargon. But *Not By Money Alone* (Jon Carpenter, £14.99) isn't a 'normal' economics book. Authors Malcolm Slesser and Jane King suggest that money is a deeply flawed concept and that – horror of horrors – the world would be a better place without it. While it does use formulae, tables and complex arguments, the writing is always readable and accessible. Any economics book which advocates burning money is worth reading!

Before the Taliban by Mary Smith (Iynx, £9.99) is a welcome addition to the volumes on Afghanistan because it concentrates on the stories of women Smith met before and after the Taliban came to power. The chapters are interconnected, often told through the women's own words. Although the slide into victimhood would be easy, Smith portrays women as actors, not re-actors within their culture. A note to Iynx: send a copy to Mr bin Laden post haste!

The latest volume in the long-running

Abertay Historical Society Series is Andrew Murray Scott's *Dundee's Literary Lives* (£12.00). Blowing the trumpet for the city by the silvery Tay, Scott's narrative waxes lyrical about its literary achievements. Although sometimes Dundee links are tenuous in the extreme, this is an enjoyable riposte to the Glasgow-Edinburgh literary hegemony.

David Purves, a former editor of *Lallans*, puts his formidable knowledge of Scots to good use in *A Scots Grammar: Scots Grammar and Usage* (Saltire Society, £9.99). In his introduction, Purves is disarmingly honest as seeing the prospects for Scots as somewhat gloomy, given the assaults on it by English, the lack of any agreed grammar and doubts over what can be legitimately regarded as Scots. The book is his attempt to counteract this by sketching out some of the main points of Scots grammar. Although a little exacting at times, it's accessible enough given the subject matter. The cartoons at the start of each section help lighten and enlighten the reader,

too. Purists may gripe that it's a little too thin, but as Purves comments, "bannoks is better nor nae breid".

'Poetry is neither rhyme, nor rhythm, nor reason' notes James Russell Grant in the perceptive introduction to his *Jigsaw and the Art of Poetry* (ELSP, £7.50). Whether wandering through industrial heartland thick with history in the epic 'Hattonrig Road', or standing in awe at 'Clydesdale Steelworks', Grant is always thoughtful and involving.

Squeezing in last is *Twentieth Century Scottish Drama* (Canongate, £12.99). A collection of plays ranging from JM Barrie to Liz Lochhead, this anthology can only be an introduction to much deeper stories. While it does have a brief introduction by editors Cairns Craig and Randall Stevenson, the book would benefit from a play or two being dropped, and some critical essays placing the plays in context added. As it stands, this is a fine, if bare, monument to Scottish theatre.

Edmund O'Connor

Notes on Contributors

Mark Barbieri was born in Govan but eventually migrated to Partick – a place which equally offers inspiration and desperation.

Martin Bates: Based in East Lothian. Edited *Poetry as a Foreign Language* (White Adder). Latest collection *Wounded Lion* (Redbeck).

Jamie Reid Baxter comes from Banffshire. Involved in 16th-17th century European cultural studies and Scotland's place therein.

Gavin Bowd: Wrote *Camouflage* (diehard, 2001) and edited *St Andrews Citizen: A Tribute to Dr Jean-Paul Marat* (Aura, 2001).

Thorbjørn Campbell: ex-civil servant and conservationist. Once longed to escape Ayrshire, now happy to be allowed to stay.

Jenni Daiches lives in South Queensferry. As 'Jenni Calder' writes on a range of subjects. Most recent book *Scots in Canada* (Luath).

Iain Galbraith's translations in *Pretext, Chicago Review, Dimensions* ... Own poems in *New Writing Scotland, Stand, P N Review*.

Thelma Good: Theatre Editor for edinburghguide.com. Helped to decide the Critics' Awards for Theatre In Scotland 2003.

Diana Hendry: Written two collections – *Making Blue* and *Borderers* (both Peterloo Poets). Wrote *Harvey Angell*, a Whitbread Award winner, and other children's books.

João Henriques: Born Portugal, studied in Edinburgh. Ex-*Chapman* volunteer, writes verses and has dog (Pinta). Now translator.

Brent Hodgson writes poetry and fiction. He has read his work to audiences in the Oxford Bar, Yellow Café and a dog kennel.

Dauvit Horsbroch: research fellow in Aberdeen, past president of Scots Language Society. Has written many papers in and on Scots.

David Kinloch teaches creative writing at Strathclyde. Poetry collections: *Paris-Forfar* (Polygon) and *Un Tour d'Ecosse* (Carcanet).

Franco Loi: Born 1930 Genoa, in Milan since 1937. Poet and critic, best known for the Milanese dialect in his politically-charged poetry.

Roddy Lumsden recently published *The Bubble Bride* (SAB/ Akros) after a residency at the St Andrews Bay Hotel. His *New & Selected Poems* (Bloodaxe) due for late 2004.

Rob Mackenzie, born 1964 Glasgow, lives with family in Turin, Italy. Poems in *Ambit, New Writing Scotland, Smiths Knoll* etc.

aonghas macneacail: Even older than *Chapman*. Much travelled, from Dead Sea to Arctic Circle. Won Society of Authors Award and Feile Filiochta Poetry Prize in 2003.

Kevin MacNeil: widely published/broadcast writer of English and Gaelic poetry, fiction and drama; first Iain Crichton Smith Fellow.

Hayden Murphy: born 1945 Dublin. Poet and arts journalist based in Edinburgh. Editor Irish Issue *Chapman* (Nos 19 and 92).

Andrew Philip lives in Linlithgow. Member of Edinburgh's Shore Poets. Awarded an SAC new writer's bursary in 2003.

David C Purdie is 62. He was a joiner, then an insurance man, retiring aged 52. Became a poet aged 50. Is still bemused.

Lydia Robb writes both poetry & prose in Scots and English. Latest poetry collection *Last Tango with Magritte* (Chapman, 2002).

Heather Scott: Born in London, has lived in Edinburgh since 1960. Has occasionally contributed poetry and prose to magazines.

Alastair Sim: trying to find publisher for first novel, *Ane Chosen Folk*. Has to work for a living, hence lack of literary output. He is 34.

Donald Smith: Poems in *Chapman, Lines Review, Poetry Scotland*. Wrote *Storytelling Scotland: A Nation in Narrative* (Polygon).

Iain Crichton Smith: now, sadly, no longer with us. Outstanding poet, novelist, playwright, unique, anarchic wit and presence. Two previously unpublished stories.

Ian Stephen is working on a Creative Scotland project – navigating through the geography of sea stories in north-west Scotland.

Raymond Vettese: First book, *The Richt Noise* (Macdonalds, 1988) won Saltire Society's Best First Book Award. Second collection *A Keen New Air* (Saltire Society, 1995).

C L Vinson, an internationally-recognised poet, has been published over 60 times. Has two unpublished collections.

Jack Withers: A message-boy I am/ A message-boy I'll remain./ The message I bring to everyone/ Is I'm not alone in being insane

Augustus Young: Latest work is *Light Years* (Menard Press/ London Magazine Editions, 2002). Also published eight books of poetry.

Chapman

Editor: Joy Hendry
Assistant Editor: Edmund O'Connor

4 Broughton Place, Edinburgh EH1 3RX, Scotland

Tel 0131–557 2207 Fax 0131–556 9565
chapman-pub@blueyonder.co.uk / www.chapman-pub.co.uk

Volunteers: Kristina Götz, Henry Harding, João Henriques,
Ann-Mhairi Pryde, Mike Stocks, M Jane Taylor

ISBN 1-903700-08-6   ISSN 0308-2695   © Chapman 2004

Chapman

Subscription Rates

	Personal		Institutional	
	1 year	2 years	1 year	2 years
UK	£18 (£13 conc*)	£34	£24 (£18 conc**)	£45
Overseas	£24/ $38	£45/ $70	£30/ $45	£52/ $84

Single issues £6 inc P&P
* Applies to students, DSS, etc
** Applies to writers' groups and similar artistic organisations
US Dollar cheques, and donations to help the work of *Chapman* welcome.

Submissions:
Chapman welcomes submissions of poetry, fiction and articles
*which **must** be accompanied by SAE or International Reply Coupons*

Scottish Arts Council

Scottish Arts Council
LOTTERY FUNDED

Production: Biddles, 24 Rollesby Road, Hardwick Industrial Estate, King's Lynn, Norfolk